PRIMARY PARTNERS
Sharing Time

The Temple

- **Learning Activities to Learn about the Temple**

- **Scripture Posters and Cards to Memorize**

- **More Teaching Tools: References to Other Learning Activities**

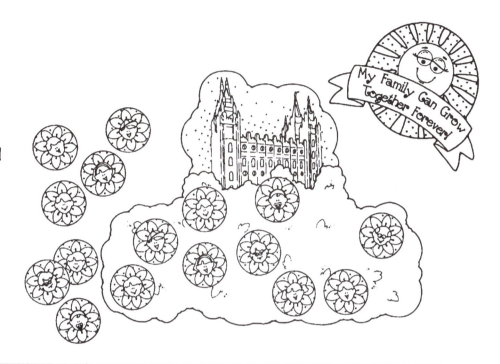

The Temple — Sharing Time Themes #1–12

1. I Love to See the Temple
2. My Family Can Be Together Forever Through the Blessings of the Temple
3. The Temple Is the House of the Lord
4. The Temple Brings the Blessings of Heaven to Earth
5. My Body Is a Temple
6. Temples Are Signs of the True Church
7. Temples Bless Heavenly Father's Children Throughout the World
8. We Serve Others Through Temple Work
9. I Will Live Now to Be Worthy to Go to the Temple and Serve a Mission
10. I Will Prepare to Go to the Temple as I Follow Heavenly Father's Plan for Me
11. I Am Thankful for Temple Blessings
12. When Jesus Comes Again, He Will Come to the Temple

Covenant Communications, Inc.
American Fork, Utah

Printed in the United States of America
First Printing: September 2001

PRIMARY PARTNERS: Sharing Time—The Temple
ISBN 1-57734-952-0

ACKNOWLEDGEMENTS: Thanks to Inspire Graphics www.inspiregraphics.com for the use of Lettering Delights computer fonts.

INTRODUCTION
The Temple: I'm Going There Someday

This volume of teaching ideas can be used year after year for Primary Sharing Time (as well as family home evening) to teach children about the temple and to increase their desire to go there someday.

These memorable activities will help children learn that:
• Through temple ordinances their family can be sealed together for eternity.
• The temple is the house of the Lord.
• Great blessings come from the temple.
• Their body is a temple.
• Temples are a sign of the true church
• Temples bless Heavenly Father's children throughout the world.
• We can serve others through temple work.
• We can learn about Heavenly Father's plan in the temple.
• When Jesus will come again and come to the temple.

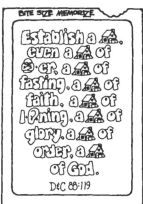

You will find **SCRIPTURES TO MEMORIZE:** Bite-size Memorize posters found in each theme section to display, and a smaller version that children can take home.

TEMPLE BOOKLET: You can help children record their thoughts and feelings about the temple by giving them an I LOVE TO SEE THE TEMPLE booklet.

1. Simply copy the label pattern shown right (on the following page).
2. Glue-mount the label on a booklet for each child.
3. Ask children to record their thoughts and feelings about the temple.
4. Ask them from time to time to share the thoughts and feelings they have recorded in the journal.
5. You may want to reward children with temple stickers to place in their journals when they share these thoughts and feelings.

GOSPEL STANDARDS WEEKLY PRESENTATION:
See Theme #1 presentation on pages 1-9 (shown right) to encourage children to keep their Gospel Standards all year. This activity is a weekly reminder.

I love to see the temple.

My thoughts and feelings about the temple.

I'm going there someday.

Name: _____

I love to see the temple.

My thoughts and feelings about the temple.

I'm going there someday.

Name: _____

MORE TEACHING TOOLS:

Add to and enhance your sharing time presentations with a second book that contains more temple activities to make learning fun. This book:

Primary Partners Sharing Time TEACHING TOOLS: The Temple

(shown right) contains over 88 activities that coordinate with The Temple Themes #1-12.

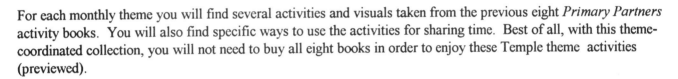

It is also available on CD-ROM to print images in full color or black and white (shown right). All of the activities in this TEACHING TOOLS book and CD-ROM are previewed in the back of this book (pages 102-117).

In this second sharing time volume (shown right), we have gathered the best TEACHING TOOLS for the 2002 The Temple sharing time theme from eight *Primary Partners* volumes.

For each monthly theme you will find several activities and visuals taken from the previous eight *Primary Partners* activity books. You will also find specific ways to use the activities for sharing time. Best of all, with this theme-coordinated collection, you will not need to buy all eight books in order to enjoy these Temple theme activities (previewed).

These activities and visuals are great for both small and large groups.
• For small sharing time groups or family home evening, copy the activities in the actual size, e.g., 8 ½" x 11" to present and give as handouts.
• For large sharing time groups, enlarge the activities to show-and-tell.

We hope you enjoy this *Primary Partners Sharing Time* book and the other two The Temple 2002 theme books:

• *Primary Partners Sharing Time Teaching Tools: The Temple* (shown above and previewed on pages 102-117).

• *Primary Partners Singing Fun!* with songs illustrated to match The Temple theme (shown right).

All are available on CD-ROM to print images in color or black and white.

TABLE OF CONTENTS

PRIMARY PARTNERS Sharing Time:
"The Temple"

THEMES #1-12:

THEME #1: I Love to See the Temple

SCRIPTURE TO MEMORIZE: Psalm 24:3-4

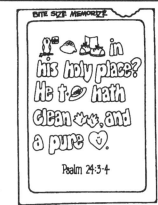

(shown right). See poster on page 2 and bite-size memorize card/handout on page 99.

LESSON: See More Teaching Tools on p. 103. <u>Ask, "Why do we love to see the temple?"</u>
Answer the question, using the scriptures, Primary lessons, and sources below to teach.
• The temple is a house of God, a place of love and beauty. I can feel the Holy Spirit there
(D&C 109:12-20; *Primary* 1, lesson 26.
• I'll go inside someday to perform sacred ordinances that will prepare me to live with
Heavenly Father again. I will make covenants and receive my endowment.
(Mosiah 5:5, *LDS Temples,* 14-19; *Primary 5,* lesson 35; *"Temple"* in the Bible Dictionary).
• I will prepare myself while I am young to go to the temple. I must have a recommend to enter
a dedicated temple (Alma 37:35; "My Gospel Standards"; *Primary 3,* lesson 3).

ACTIVITIES: I Will Stand in Holy Places
(I'm Going There Someday—Gospel Standards Review)

OBJECTIVE: Help children make a commitment to live the Gospel Standards so they can one day "stand in holy places" and enter the temple to do a sacred work.

HANDOUT: My Gospel Standards doorknob sign (shown left), for activity below.

TO MAKE: (1) *Copy, color, and cut out a My Gospel Standards doorknob sign (page 3) for each child.
(2) Laminate for durability if desired. Or, simply print the doorknob signs from the CD-ROM in color.
See Introduction for details.

GOSPEL STANDARDS PRESENTATION: Make a poster of the temple. Have children post a
boy or girl image on the temple grounds to show they are standing in holy places. Tell children that if they
live the Gospel Standards each day they will be worthy to enter the temple.

TO MAKE: (1) *Copy, color, and cut out, and laminate the
temple, temple grounds, and I'm Going to the Temple Someday
sign (pages 4-5). Post on a large poster or laminate posterboard
after pieces have been posted. (2) *Copy, color, and cut out a boy
or girl image (pages 8-9) for each child in the Primary. Divide
images according to classes and write the name of each child on the
image. Give these to the teachers as they arrive.

ACTIVITY:
1. Tell children that if they live the Gospel Standards they can be
worthy to stand in holy places and attend the temple someday.
They can see the beauty inside and feel the peace therein. They
can go there to learn of Heavenly Father's plan for them and feel
the Holy Spirit. They can go there for special guidance and
direction as they do the sacred work that is needed there. They can
be baptized and do endowment and sealings there for those who
have passed on and are not able to perform the work for themselves.
2. Review the Gospel Standards by giving each child a Gospel Standards doorknob sign. Have children take turns reading
them aloud. Encourage children to post on their doorknob as a reminder.
3. Have children come up as a class and say "I love to see the temple, I'm going there someday," and post their image on
the poster with double-stick tape. Tell them that by doing this, they are making a commitment to live the Gospel Standards
and prepare for the temple.

WEEKLY REVIEW: Have one or two children each week to come up and tell how they have been living a certain Gospel
Standard. Read the gospel standard and have children tell of their experiences. They can find their image on the poster to
hold, saying, "I will live the Gospel Standards so I can stand in holy places."

*All images can be printed in full-color or black and white with the *Primary Partners Sharing Time: The Temple* CD-ROM.

Psalm 24:3-4

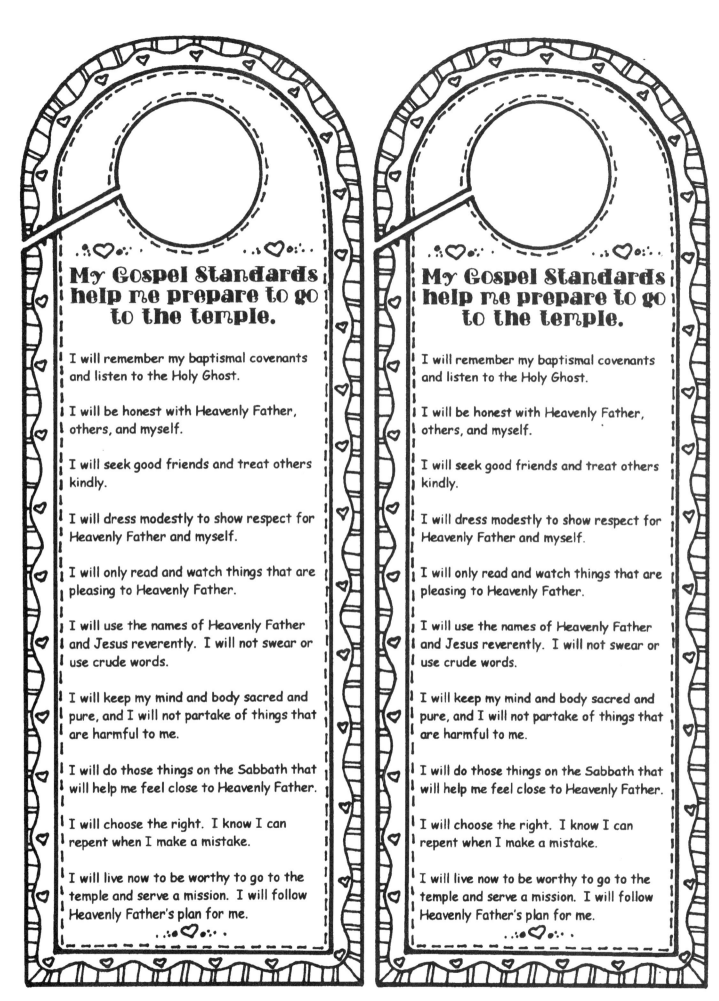

My Gospel Standards help me prepare to go to the temple.

I will remember my baptismal covenants and listen to the Holy Ghost.

I will be honest with Heavenly Father, others, and myself.

I will seek good friends and treat others kindly.

I will dress modestly to show respect for Heavenly Father and myself.

I will only read and watch things that are pleasing to Heavenly Father.

I will use the names of Heavenly Father and Jesus reverently. I will not swear or use crude words.

I will keep my mind and body sacred and pure, and I will not partake of things that are harmful to me.

I will do those things on the Sabbath that will help me feel close to Heavenly Father.

I will choose the right. I know I can repent when I make a mistake.

I will live now to be worthy to go to the temple and serve a mission. I will follow Heavenly Father's plan for me.

My Gospel Standards help me prepare to go to the temple.

I will remember my baptismal covenants and listen to the Holy Ghost.

I will be honest with Heavenly Father, others, and myself.

I will seek good friends and treat others kindly.

I will dress modestly to show respect for Heavenly Father and myself.

I will only read and watch things that are pleasing to Heavenly Father.

I will use the names of Heavenly Father and Jesus reverently. I will not swear or use crude words.

I will keep my mind and body sacred and pure, and I will not partake of things that are harmful to me.

I will do those things on the Sabbath that will help me feel close to Heavenly Father.

I will choose the right. I know I can repent when I make a mistake.

I will live now to be worthy to go to the temple and serve a mission. I will follow Heavenly Father's plan for me.

I'm Going to the Temple Someday.

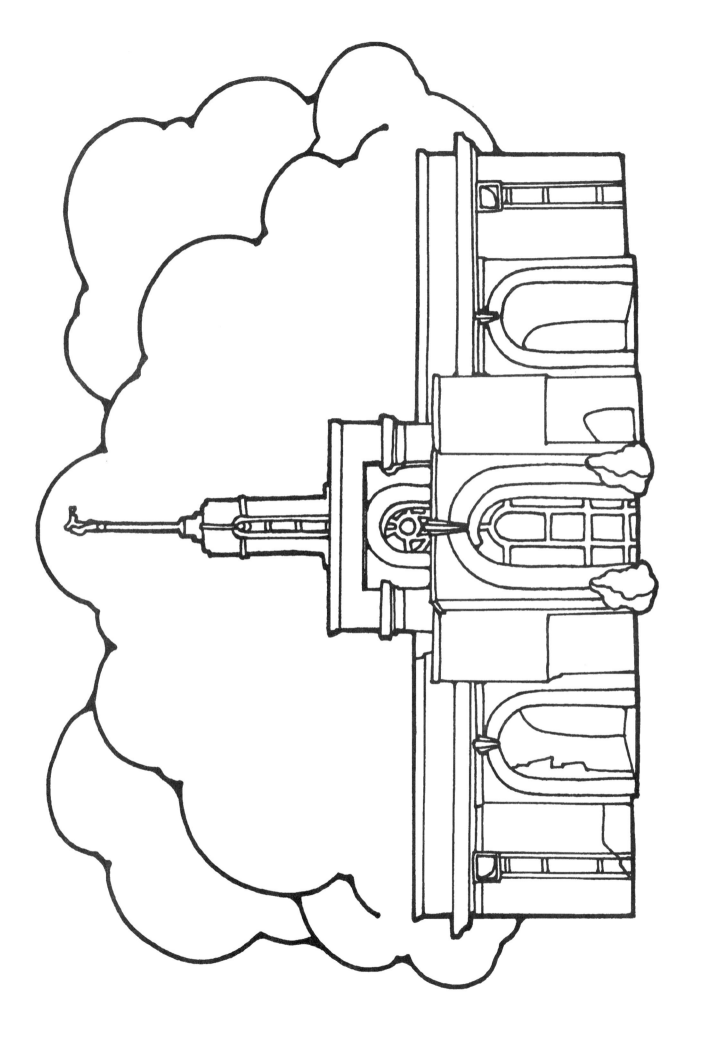

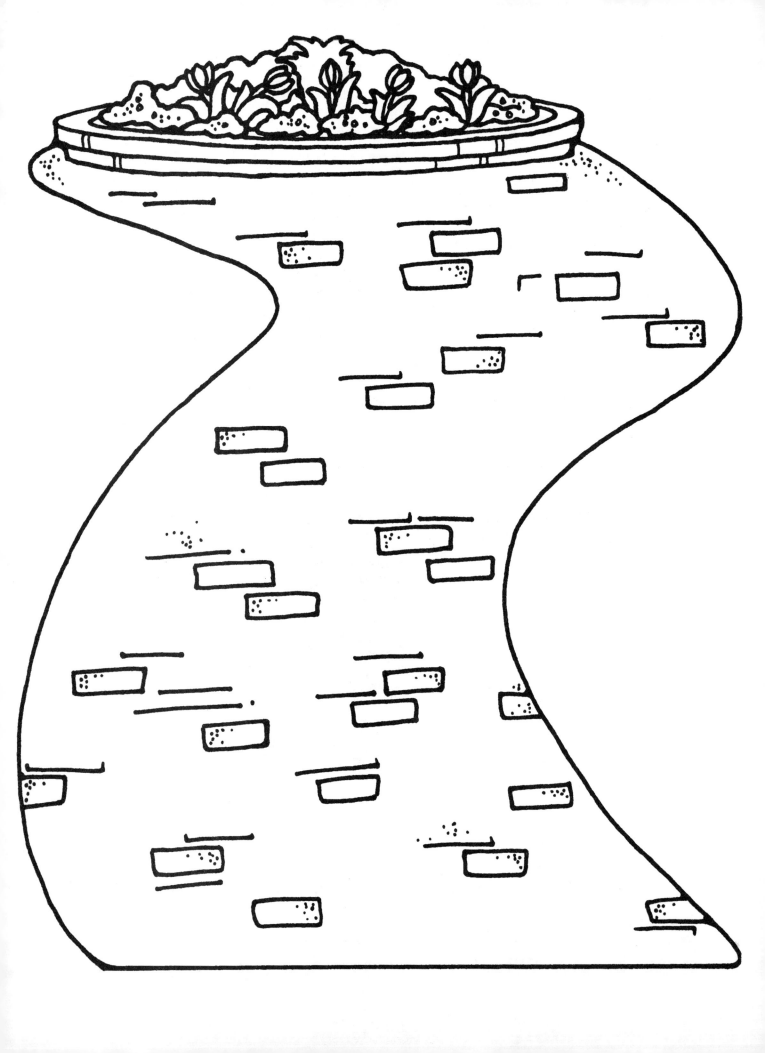

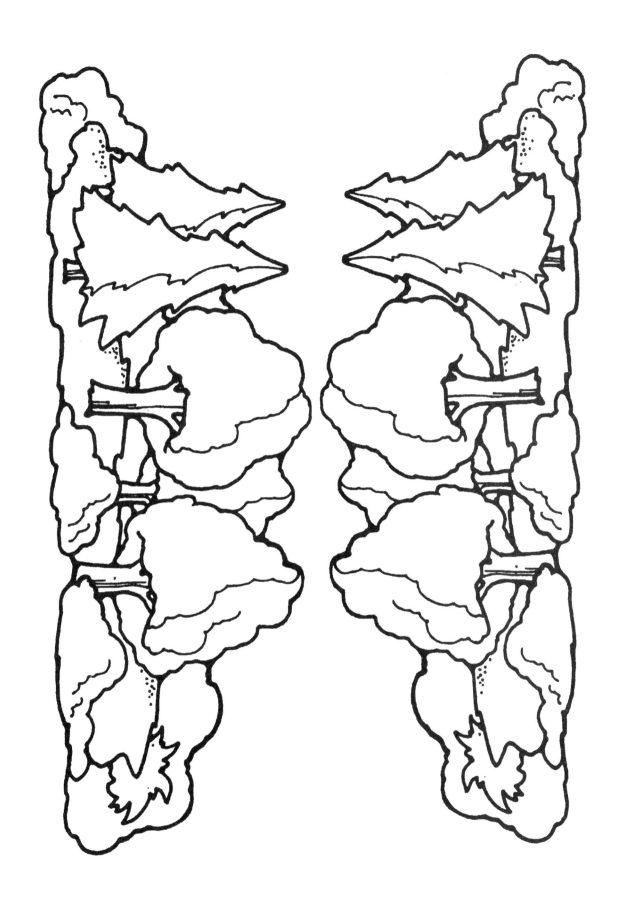

THEME #2: My Family Can Be Together Forever Through the Blessings of the Temple

BITE SIZE MEMORIZE

And give N2 thee the of the dom of : and whatsoever thou shalt on in .

Matthew 16:19

SCRIPTURE TO MEMORIZE: Matthew 16:19

(shown right). See poster on page 11 and bite-size memorize card/handout on page 99.

LESSON: See More Teaching Tools on page 103. <u>Ask, "How can families be together forever through the blessings of the temple?"</u> Answer the question using the scriptures, Primary lessons, and other sources (below) to teach.

• In the temple my family can be sealed together forever. Marriage in the temple is for eternity (D&C 132:19; *Gospel Principles*, chapter 38; *Primary 3*, lesson 35 (enrichment activity 1)).

• Temple ordinances are performed by priesthood authority (D&C 132:45-49; *Primary 5*, lesson 26, *LDS Temples*, 23-26).

• My family can live to be worthy of the blessings of the temple. Love grows in my family as we have family home evening, family prayer, and family scripture study, and as we serve one another (Mosiah 4:14-15; *The Family: A Proclamation to the World*; *Gospel Principles*, chapters 36, 37; *Primary 4*, less. 26; *LDS Temples*, 23-26).

ACTIVITY: I Can Help My Family Grow Together Forever (Planting Faithful Flowers)

OBJECTIVE: Increase children's desire to be worthy of temple blessings by having their family's love grow. They can plant faithful flowers on the temple grounds to help their family grow together forever. The faithful flowers show ways love grows in their family as they have family home evening, family prayer, family scripture study, and serving one another.

TO MAKE:

1. *Copy, color, and cut out images and wordstrips (pages 12-17). You'll need 3 copies of the family flower page.

2. To make faithful flowers, glue a wordstrip on the back of each flower, laminate, and place in a container.

3. Mount My Family Can Grow Together Forever! sign, temple, and temple grounds on a poster. Laminate for durability.

4. Set up. Faithful flowers can be drawn from a container or hidden around the room, e.g., taped under chairs or to the walls.

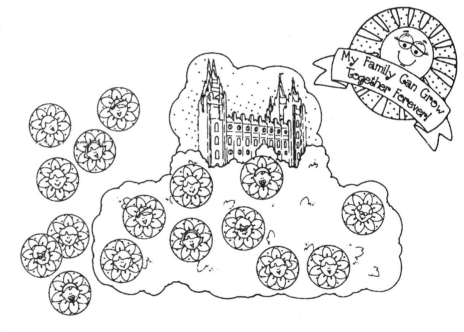

ACTIVITY: Say, "If we are faithful with our family in keeping the commandments, we can prepare to go to the temple." Point to the sun and have a child read the sign, "My Family Can Grow Together Forever!" Tell children that the sun represents the celestial kingdom where families can live together forever through obedience to gospel principles. Say, "When you go the temple gardens you see beautiful flowers. We too can plant beautiful flowers in our family's garden by helping our family's love grow. Let's learn how."

1. Have children find the flowers hidden in the room. They can also take turns drawing flowers from a container to read.

2. Turn the flowers over one by one and talk about each action that helps a family's love to grow.

3. Place the flower on the temple gardens with double-stick tape.

*All images can be printed in full-color or black and white with the *Primary Partners Sharing Time: The Temple* CD-ROM.

And  give N2 thee the 🔑 of the 👷+dom of ☁: and whatsoever thou shalt 🐝 on 🌎 🍞 🐝 🐝 in ☁.

Matthew 16:19

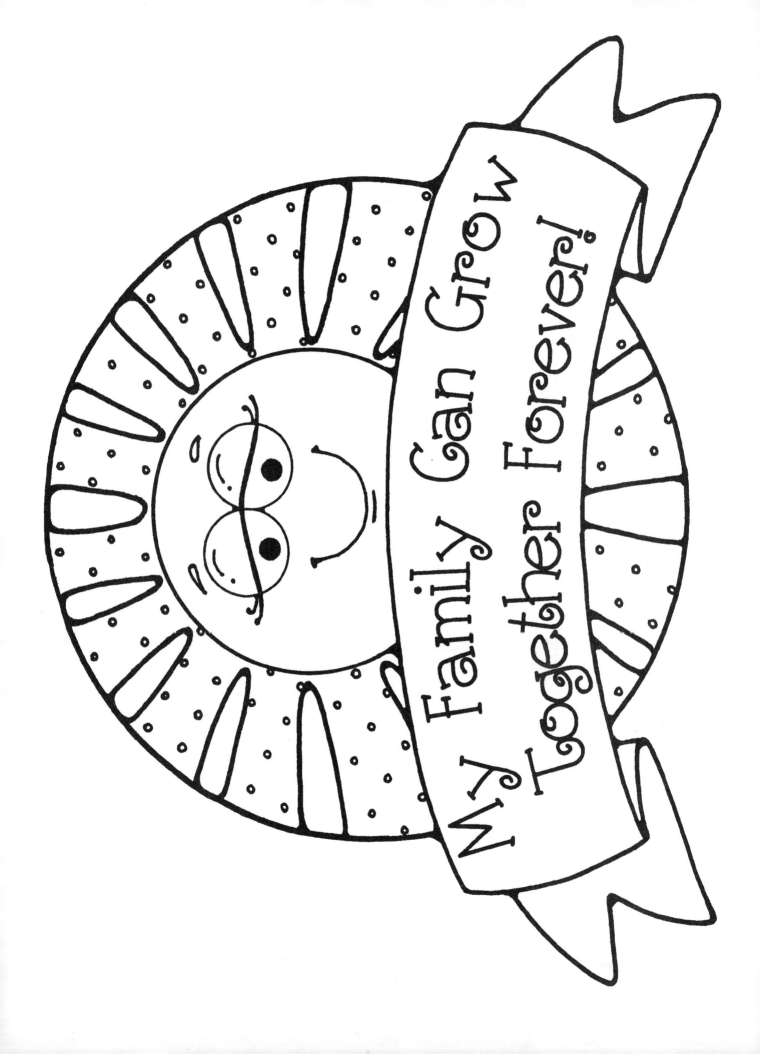

My Family Can Grow Together Forever!

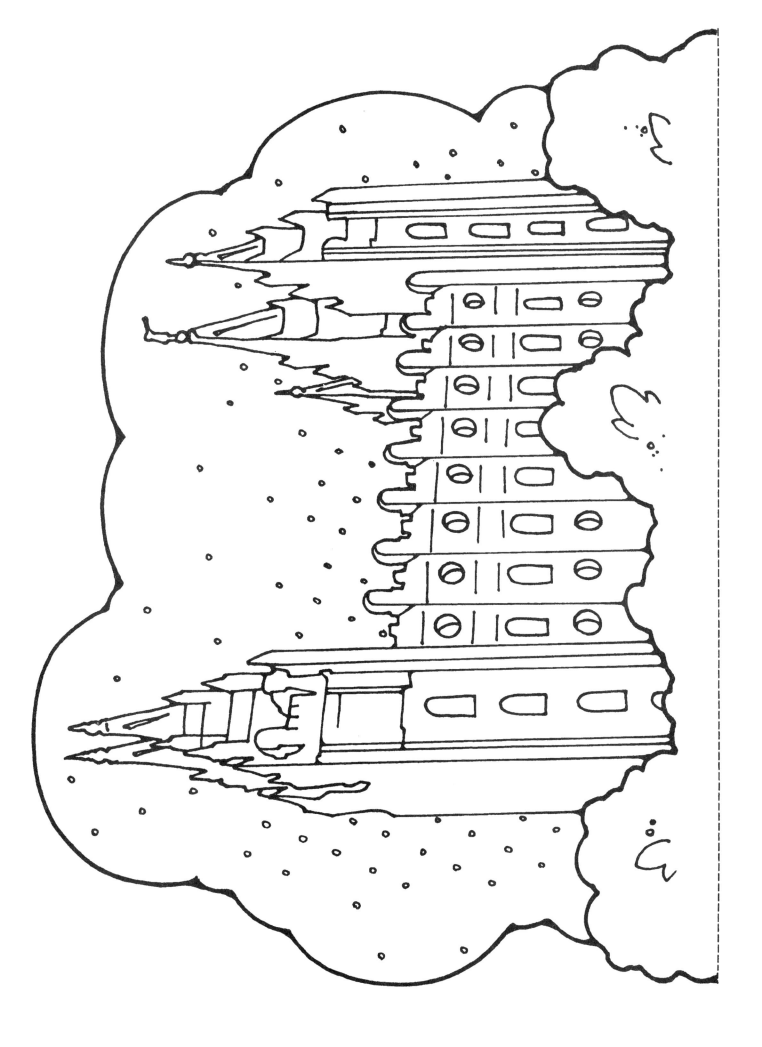

I can remind my family to have family home evening.

I can get my family together for family prayer.

I can get my family out of bed in the morning for scripture study.

I can serve my family by making their beds.

I can smile as I help Mom with the dishes.

I can show my baby brother love by playing with him.

I can help keep my baby sister safe while playing in the yard.

I can read scripture stories to my younger brother who can't read.

I can prepare the treat for family home evening.

I can plan a family home evening and give everyone a part.

I can find scriptures to read in family home evening.

I can say "please" and "thank you."

I can cheer up my sister when she is sad.

I can make a list of things I want our family to pray about.

I can help my dad when he comes home tired. I will get him something cool to drink.

I can read about the Book of Mormon heros to my family.

I can watch my baby brother so he won't get into things.

I can keep peace in my family by helping others not to fight.

I can set an example for my sister and say my prayer when I wake up.

I can show my love by giving out hugs.

I can read the *Friend* magazine with my brother and sister.

I can memorize scriptures with Dad.

I can play games with my family each week.

I can be ready when it's time for family prayer.

I can prepare and give the lesson in family home evening.

I can make my grandpa happy by playing games with him or calling him on the phone.

THEME #3: The Temple Is the House of the Lord

SCRIPTURE TO MEMORIZE: D&C 88:119 (shown right).

See poster on page 19 and bite-size memorize card/handout on page 99.
See Step #5 below to present.

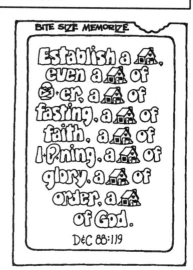

LESSON: See More Teaching Tools on page 105. <u>Ask, "How is the temple the house of the Lord?"</u> Answer the question using the scriptures, Primary lessons, and other sources (below) to teach.

• When Jesus lived on the earth, He came to the temple in Jerusalem (Luke 2:22-52; John 8:2; *Primary 7*, lessons 5, 8).
• After His resurrection, the Savior came to the Nephite temple in the land Bountiful. He taught and blessed the people there (3 Nephi 11; *Primary 4*, lessons 33, 35).
• When the Savior comes to earth, He often comes to a temple. We can feel His Spirit there (D&C 110:1-10; 97:15-16; 109:5; *Primary 1*, lesson 26, account of Lorenzo Snow).

ACTIVITY: The Temple Is the House of God
(Building a House of God show-and-tell)

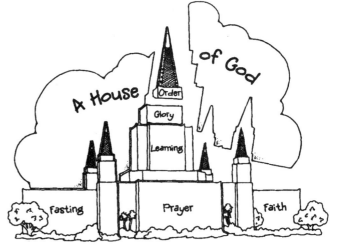

OBJECTIVE: Help children learn the scripture D&C 88:119 (shown above) to understand why the temple is a house of prayer, fasting, faith, learning, glory, and order. Teach them why this is necessary for the Savior to enter and for the Spirit to be there. This also applies to the atmosphere of our church meeting house and our individual homes.

TO MAKE:

1. *Copy, color, and cut out "A House of God" clouds and temple block wordstrips: Fasting, Prayer, Faith, Learning, Glory, and Order (pages 20-24).
2. Position clouds on posterboard or chalkboard ready for other wordstrip pieces to be placed.
3. Place double-stick tape on the back of each wordstrip and give to teachers during activity (see step #7 below).

ACTIVITY: Spend 5 minutes on #1-5 and 10 minutes on #6-8.

1. Place a fancy chair in front of children. Tell them that we are going to pretend we have a special guest visiting us today, sitting in this chair. Who might this special guest be?
2. <u>Show a picture of a ward meetinghouse.</u> Talk to children about how they would feel if the Savior came to their Primary today. Ask, "Would you be noisy? Would you throw paper on the floor? Would you not fold your arms during the prayer and listen to the lessons taught? Would you be reverent? Would you run down the hall? How would you act? What would you do if the Savior come to their Primary today?"
3. <u>Show a picture of a temple</u> and ask, "If the Savior were to come to his temple today, how would you act?"
4. Review the D&C 88:119 poster (shown above).
5. Ask children to help you build a house of God where Jesus would feel welcome.
6. Divide children into six different groups. Give each group a temple puzzle piece with the wordstrips that match the subject, e.g., give the faith wordstrips to the group you give the faith temple puzzle piece. Have the groups take 2-3 minutes to decide what they will tell about the their temple block. Children can read from the wordstrips and share ideas.
7. Build "A House of God" by posting the sign on the board. Have children from each group come up and place the block on the board to build the temple and tell why this action is important, reading the wordstrips or their own ideas. Build in this order: Fasting, Prayer, Faith, Learning, Glory, and Order.

    *All images can be printed in full-color or black and white with the *Primary Partners Sharing Time: The Temple* CD-ROM.

Establish a 🏠, even a 🏠 of prayer, a 🏠 of fasting, a 🏠 of faith, a 🏠 of learning, a 🏠 of glory, a 🏠 of order, a 🏠 of God.

D&C 88:119

A House

FASTING increases our faith and helps us feel closer to Heavenly Father and Jesus.

FASTING helps us pray for special blessings.

FASTING and prayer help us know that things are true by the spirit of revelation.

FASTING should include the paying of fast offerings to help the poor and needy.

FASTING helps us to be humble and teachable.

FASTING opens our mind and heart to obtain knowledge.

PRAYER: Our sincere prayers keep us safe and help us resist temptation.

PRAYER: Heavenly Father is pleased when we thank Him in our prayers.

PRAYER and fasting bring blessings into our lives, and the lives of those we pray for.

PRAYER: We pray for forgiveness and for help to keep the commandments.

PRAYER: Through prayer, we can talk directly to our Heavenly Father.

PRAYER: Heavenly Father always listens to and hears our prayers.

PRAYER: We are commanded to "pray always."

PRAYER: We should always to pray "in the name of Jesus Christ."

PRAYER: We pray to bless the sick, our families, the prophet, and the missionaries.

PRAYER: Our prayers bring Heavenly Father's blessings in to our lives.

FAITH is *"hope for things which are not seen, which are true."*

FAITH in Jesus Christ's teachings can lead us back to live with Heavenly Father.

FAITH can increase as we study the scriptures and live the gospel.

FAITH brings miracles and blessings.

FAITH makes it possible for us to be healed by priesthood power.

FAITH helps us understand the work and word of God.

LEARNING: We can learn about Heavenly Father's plan.

LEARNING: I have learned that families can be together forever through temple ordinances.

LEARNING: We can learn what we need to do to live with Heavenly Father and Jesus again.

LEARNING: I can learn about Heavenly Father's world and His creations.

GLORY: The temple teaches us how we can obtain eternal life, life with Heavenly Father and Jesus.

GLORY: We are of royal birth as we are children of our Heavenly Father. We are princes and princesses.

GLORY: We can become like God someday and live as He does.

GLORY: As we keep the commandments we can be part of Heavenly Father's kingdom forever.

ORDER: The temple helps us receive priesthood ordinances that will help us enter into the kingdom of God.

ORDER: Everyone must be worthy to enter the temple by living the commandments.

ORDER: If we follow Heavenly Father's plan, we can have the same blessings He has. We can become like Him.

THEME #4: The Temple Brings the Blessings of Heaven to Earth

SCRIPTURE TO MEMORIZE: D&C 14:7 (shown right).
See poster on page 26 and bite-size memorize card/handout on page 99.

LESSON: See More Teaching Tools on page 106. <u>Ask, "How can the temple bring blessings of heaven to the earth?"</u> Answer the question using the scriptures, Primary lessons, and other sources (below) to teach.
• The temple teaches us Heavenly Father's plan of salvation (*Gospel Principles*, chapter 47; *Primary* 1, lesson 3).
• The temple is a house of learning and inspiration (D&C 97:10-16; *Primary 5, lesson 26)*.
• A picture of the temple reminds me I am a child of God. If I keep the commandments, I can live with Him someday (Romans 8:16-17; *Primary* 6, lesson 12, enrichment activity 6).

ACTIVITY: I Treasure Temple Blessings
(Temple Treasures Hunt)

OBJECTIVE: Children find jewels that tell about the temple. They can learn of the blessings of heaven that the temple brings to earth. This will increase their desire to live so they can be worthy to go to the temple and receive these blessings.

TO MAKE:
1. *Copy, color, and cut out the Temple Treasures chest and jewels (pages 27-30).
2. *Copy, color, and cut out four jewel pages (page 31) to make 16 jewels.
3. Glue-mount a wordstrip on the back of each jewel.
4. Laminate treasure chest and jewels.
5. Cut out images after laminating, cutting a slit above the treasure chest (to mount jewels during the activity).
6. Glue the bottom portion of the treasure box on the sides and bottom, leaving the pocket open to insert jewels.
7. Hide jewels around the room.

ACTIVITY: Tell children that the temple brings the blessings of heaven to earth. Say, "Let's reach inside this Temple Treasures chest to find temple jewels, or blessings that the temple brings.
1. Have children go on a treasure hunt to find the jewels (taped on the wall, under chairs, etc.).
2. Have children take turns reading aloud from the jewels they have found, then place them in the Temple Treasures chest.
3. If there is time, read from the jewels again and talk about them.

*All images can be printed in full-color or black and white with the *Primary Partners Sharing Time: The Temple* CD-ROM.

And, if U [key] + p m + [eye] [tablets] and N + dure 2 the end U [seed] have eternal life, which [gift] is the greatest of all the [gift]s of God.

D&C 14:7

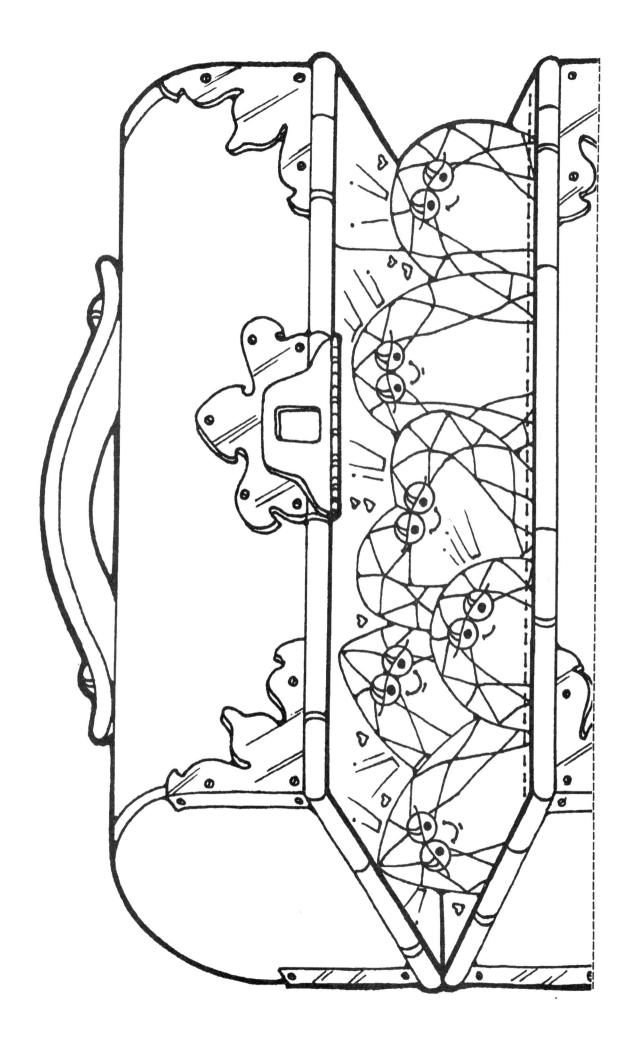

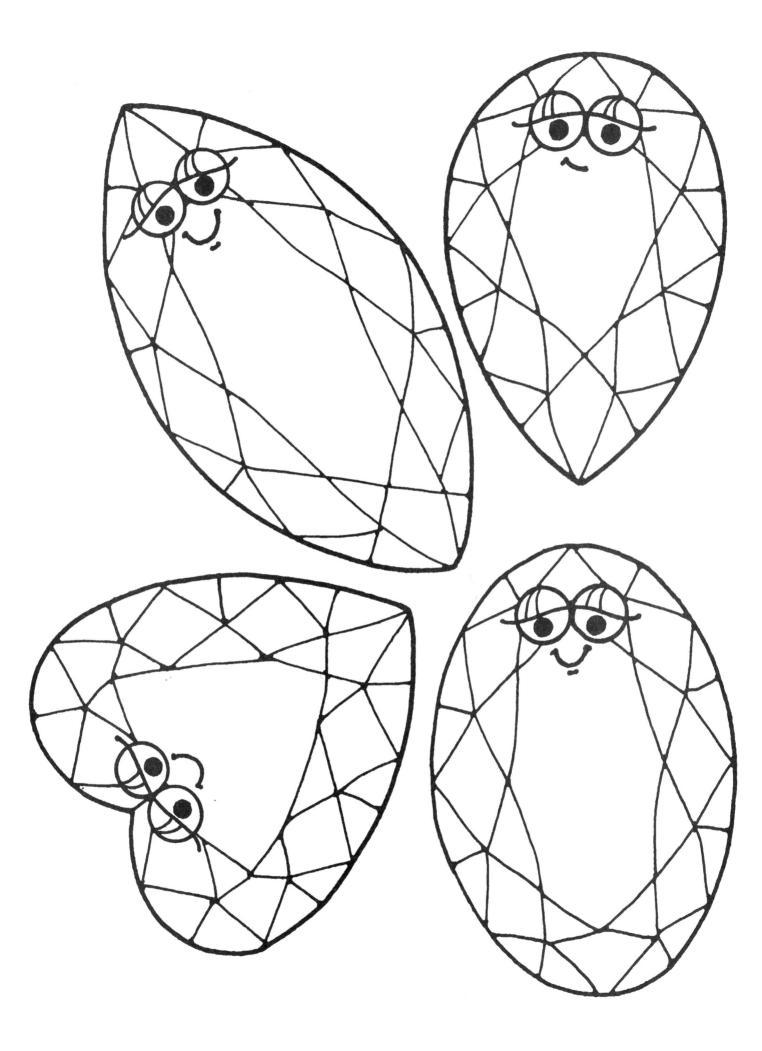

In the temple I learn that I am Heavenly Father's child and that I lived in His presence.

In the temple I learn about the choice we made to follow Jesus.

In the temple I learn I must be obedient to return to Heavenly Father's presence.

In the temple I learn that husbands and wives must love and care for each other.

In the temple I learn of the creation of the world.

When I came to earth, a veil was placed over my mind so I would not remember my life there. The temple teaches me about my heavenly home.

In the temple I learn that Heavenly Father loves us and will help us make right choices.

In the temple I learn that Jesus is our special brother.

The temple teaches me that Jesus sacrificed His life so we can return to Heavenly Father.

The temple teaches me that this life is a test to see if we will be obedient to all Heavenly Father's commandments.

In the temple I learn that Heavenly Father cares for me and wants me to return to Him.

The temple teaches me the purpose of life: where I came from, why I am here on earth, and where I am going.

The temple teaches me about the three degrees of glory and that the celestial kingdom is the highest, where God dwells. I can go there if I am worthy.

The temple teaches me that God wants me to be like Him and share in His happiness.

The temple teaches me that I can have my righteous family members with me forever.

The temple teaches me that Satan wants me to make wrong choices and will try to deceive me.

THEME #5: My Body Is a Temple

SCRIPTURE TO MEMORIZE: | 1 Corinthians 3:16-17 |

(shown right). See poster on page 33 and bite-size memorize card/handout on page 100.

LESSON: See More Teaching Tools on page 107. <u>Ask, "How can we keep our body sacred and pure, as our body is a temple?"</u> Answer the question using the scriptures, Primary lessons, and other sources (below) to teach.

• I will keep my mind and body sacred and pure, and I will not partake of things that are harmful to me (*Primary* 3, lesson 14; *Primary* 5, lesson 24, enrichment activities).

• I will only listen to music that is pleasing to Heavenly Father. I will only read and watch things that are pleasing to Heavenly Father (*Primary* 3, lesson 38; *Primary* 6, lesson 16, enrichment activities).

• I will use the names of Heavenly Father and Jesus reverently. I will not swear or use crude words (Exodus 20:7; *Primary* 3, lesson 43; *Primary* 7, lesson 41). I will dress modestly to show respect for Heavenly Father and myself (*Primary* 5, lesson 44, enrichment activity 2).

ACTIVITY: My Body Is Sacred Like the Temple
(good and bad choices match)

OBJECTIVE: Help children learn about choices they can make to keep their body sacred and pure like the temple.

TO MAKE: (1) *Copy, color, and cut out girl and boy three-part poster, garbage can, and images (pages 34-41). (2) Tape girl and boy poster together. Laminate poster and garbage can. (3) Laminate images, cut out, and place in a container to draw from. (4) Use double-stick tape to post.

ACTIVITY: Post and do steps 1-4 or play game (below*).

1. <u>Place boy and girl poster on board</u> and say the following.

• "The temple is the house of God, a sacred and pure place where Heavenly Father, Jesus, and the Holy Ghost visit. Does Heavenly Father let unworthy people enter the temple? Some would not be reverent or don't keep the commandments. Those who do are not allowed to enter the temple. Those who are willing to keep all of Heavenly Father's commandments can enter this sacred place.

• Just as bad people are not allowed to enter the temple, we don't want bad things enter our body or mind. Our body is a sacred place like the temple, where the Holy Ghost can dwell.

• Because our body is a temple, we want to keep our mind and body sacred and pure. We do not want to partake of things that are harmful. The Holy Ghost cannot dwell in an unclean place. We will be blessed with health and happiness if we put into our mind and body good things."

2. <u>Place the garbage can next to the boy and girl poster.</u>

• Say, "What do we need to avoid to keep our mind and body pure? What is considered trash, and does not belong in our mind or body? What things do we let enter our mind and body?"

• Have children come up one at a time, draw an image from the container, and read it aloud. Place the image next to the girl and boy or the garbage can with tape. Images can be placed by the body parts, e.g.: "Listen to good music" is placed by the ear, "Use good language" placed by the mouth, "Eat good food" placed by the stomach."

3. <u>Take down the garbage can and wrong choice images</u> and say "We want to keep our body as a temple by avoiding the things that make our body and spirit weak. Some say, 'Just try it. It won't hurt you.' What do you say? 'No.'"

4. <u>Point to the good choices</u> and review. Say, "Only good things should go into the temple and into our body, which is a temple for our spirits."

GAME OPTION: Children can divide into teams. Teams take turns drawing and posting images on the board next to the body (giving one point) or next to the garbage (no points) to determine winning team.

*All images can be printed in full-color or black and white with the *Primary Partners Sharing Time: The Temple* CD-ROM.

Know ye not to ye R the temple of God, and to the Spirit of God dwelleth in U? ...4 the temple of God is holy, which temple ye R.

1 Cor. 3:16-17

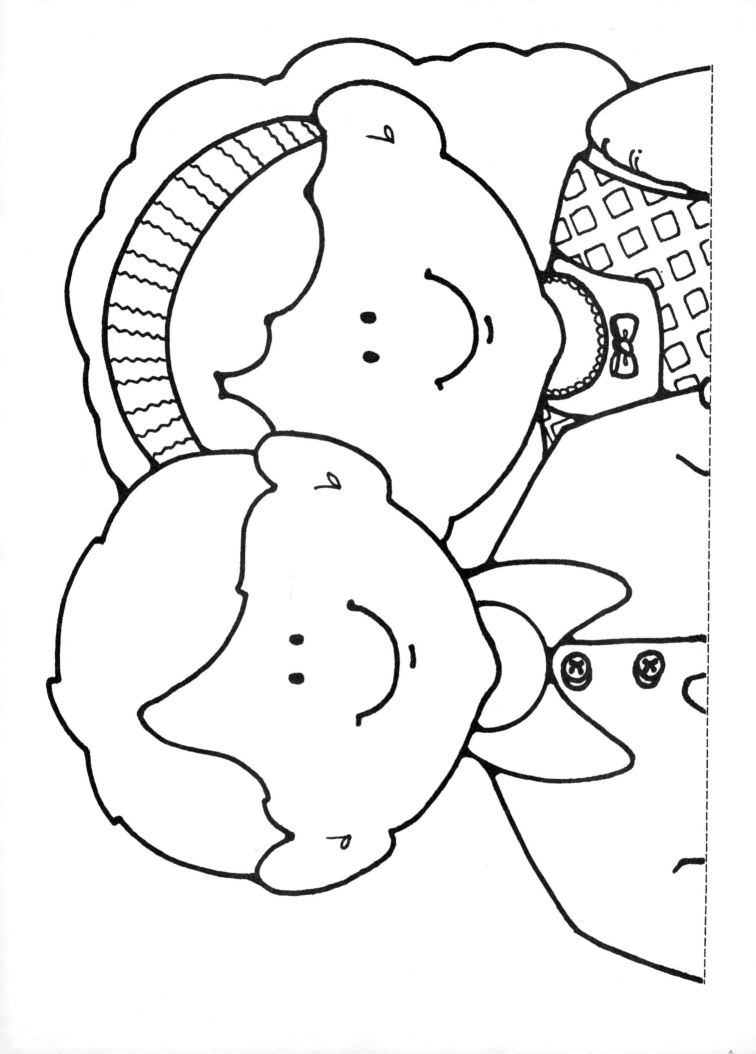

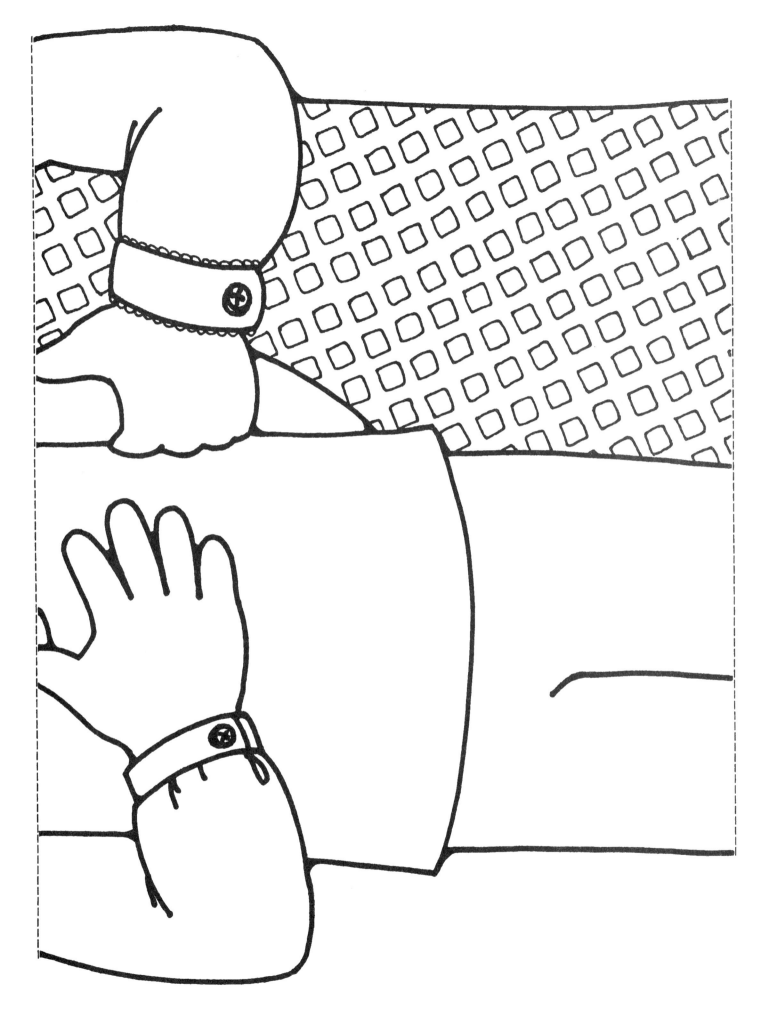

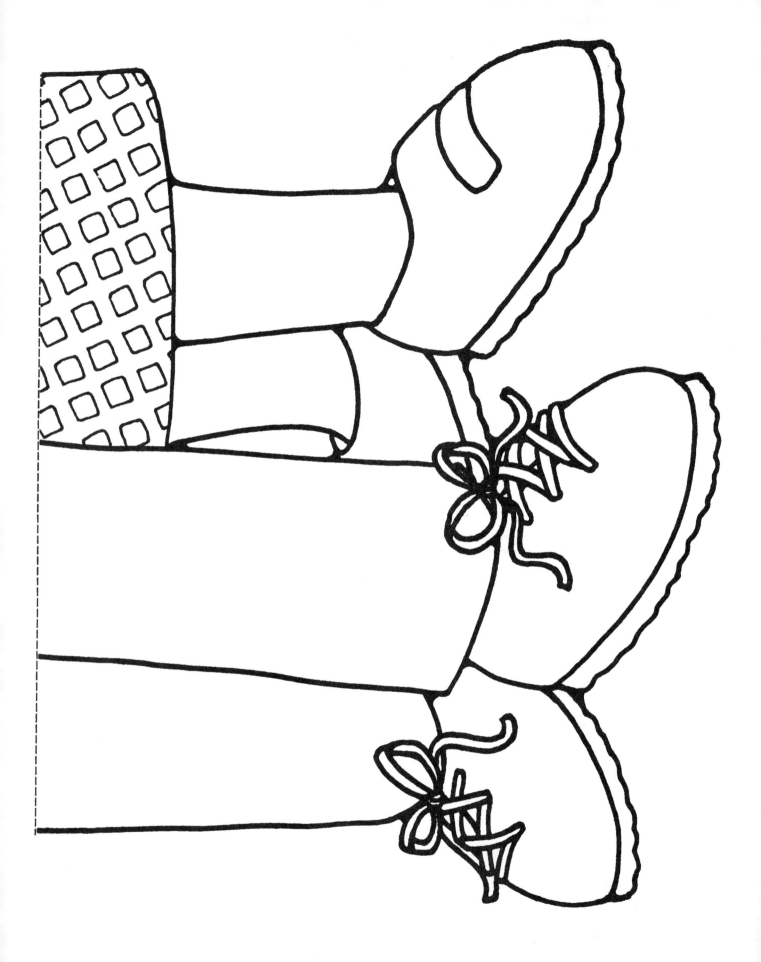

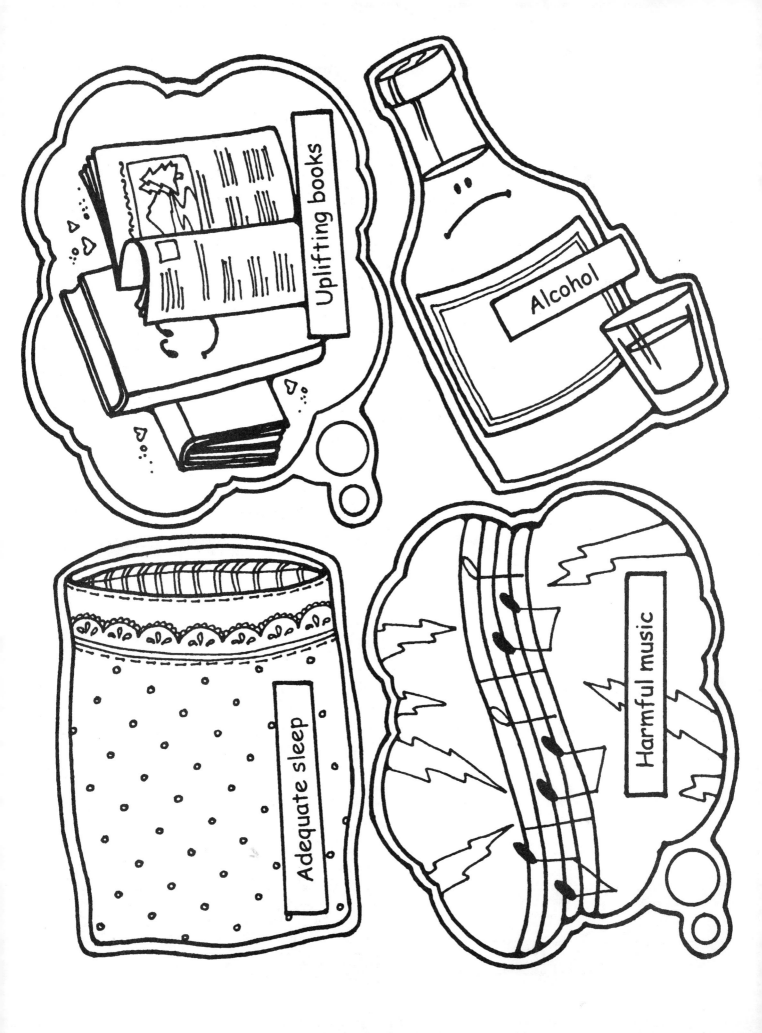

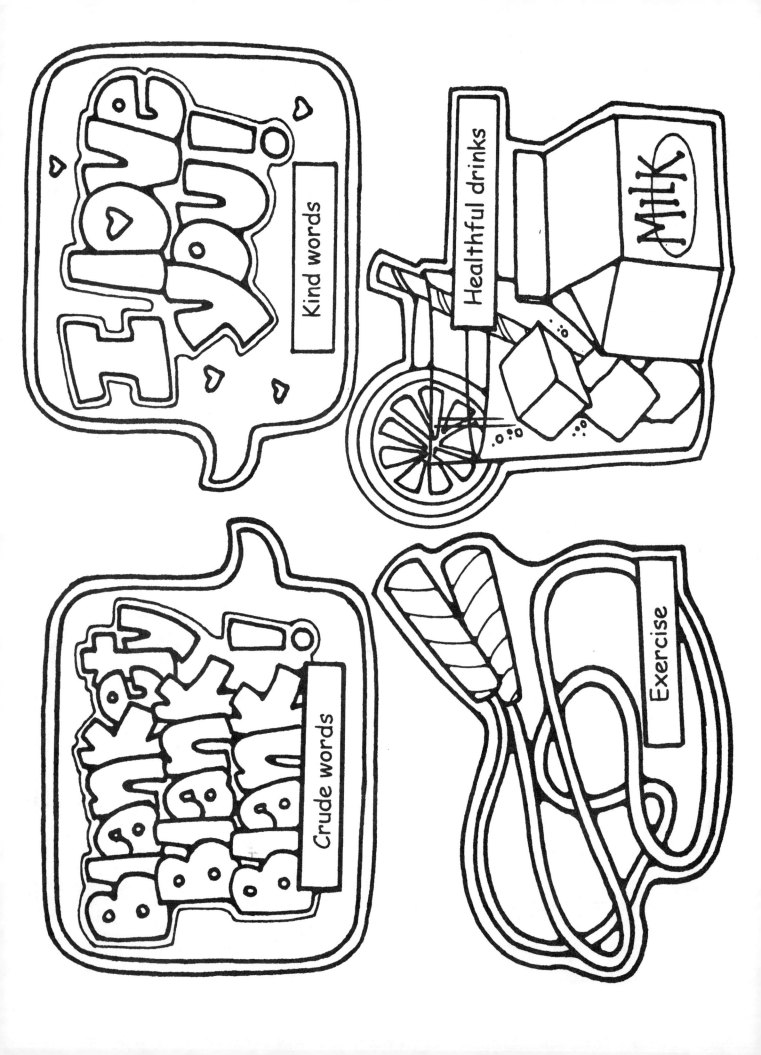

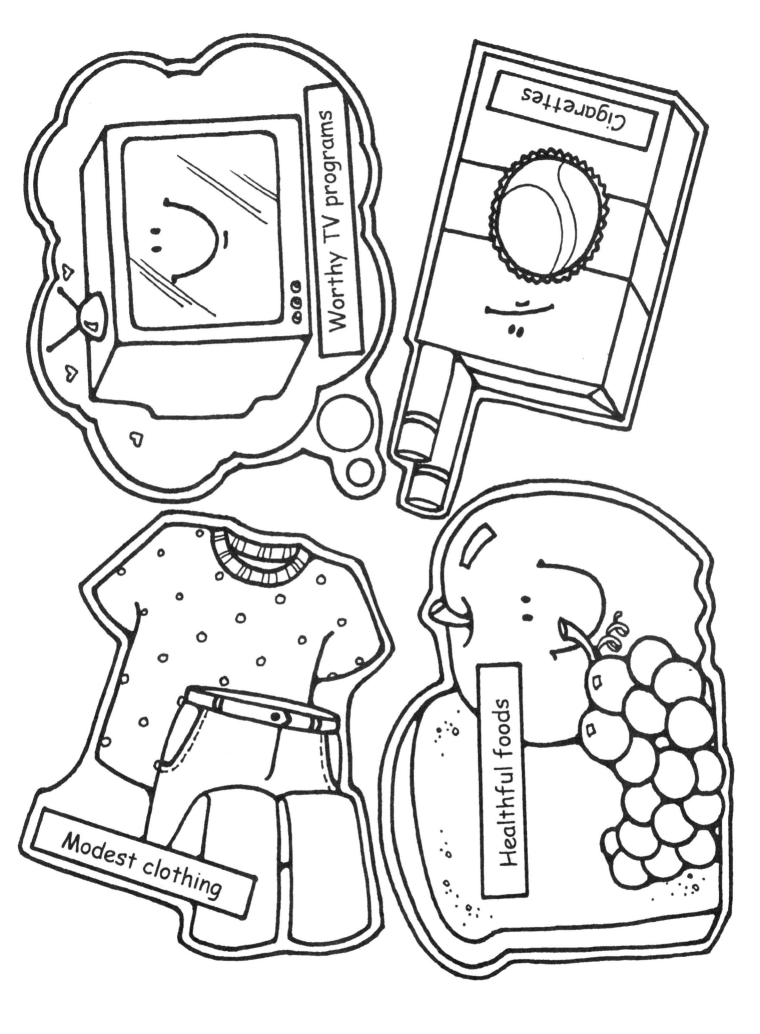

THEME #6: Temples Are Signs of the True Church

SCRIPTURE TO MEMORIZE: D&C 124:31

(shown right). See poster on page 43 and bite-size memorize card/handout on p. 100.

LESSON: See More Teaching Tools on page 108. <u>Ask, "Why are temples a sign of the true church?"</u> Answer the question using the scriptures, Primary lessons, and other sources (below) to teach.

• Moses and the children of Israel had a tabernacle, a temple they carried with them (*LDS Temples*, 52-61; Exodus 33:7; D&C 124:38; "Tabernacle" in the Bible Dictionary). Solomon built a temple in Jerusalem (1 Kings 6:1; *Primary 6*, lesson 31).
• The Nephites had temples (2 Nephi 5:16; Jacob 1:17; Mosiah 2:1-7; 3 Nephi 11:1)
• Joseph Smith restored temple blessings in the latter days (D&C 124:39-40; *Primary 5*, lesson 25, 26, 35).

BITE SIZE MEMORIZE

👄 command☞ U, all ye my saints, 2 build a 🏠 N2 me.

D&C 124:31

ACTIVITY: Ancient and Latter-day Temples (Temples Through Time puppet show)

OBJECTIVE: Help children learn that temples are signs of the true church. This activity helps children learn about the ancient temples built by Moses, King Solomon, and Nephi. Children will also learn how Joseph Smith received revelation to build the first temples in modern times.

TO MAKE:
1. *Copy, color, and cut out the prophet and king puppets, temples, and cue cards (pages 44-49).
2. Laminate images and place a wide wooden craft stick on the back of each.

ACTIVITY:
1. Ask eight children to help you present this, giving each a prophet or king puppet, or temple.
2. Have each child hold the prophet or king puppet in one hand and the temple in the

other hand, holding onto the stick (or holding onto the images without the sticks attached).
3. Show one set (prophet and temple) at a time in this order while reading the cue cards: Moses and the tabernacle, Solomon and the temple, Nephi and the temple, and Joseph Smith and Kirtland Temple.
4. Then mix up children's positions by having children change positions and images.
5. Read the cue cards again, having the other children find and line up the prophet and king puppets with their temples in the chronological order (detailed in #3 and shown above).

*All images can be printed in full-color or black and white with the *Primary Partners Sharing Time: The Temple* CD-ROM.

D&C 124:31

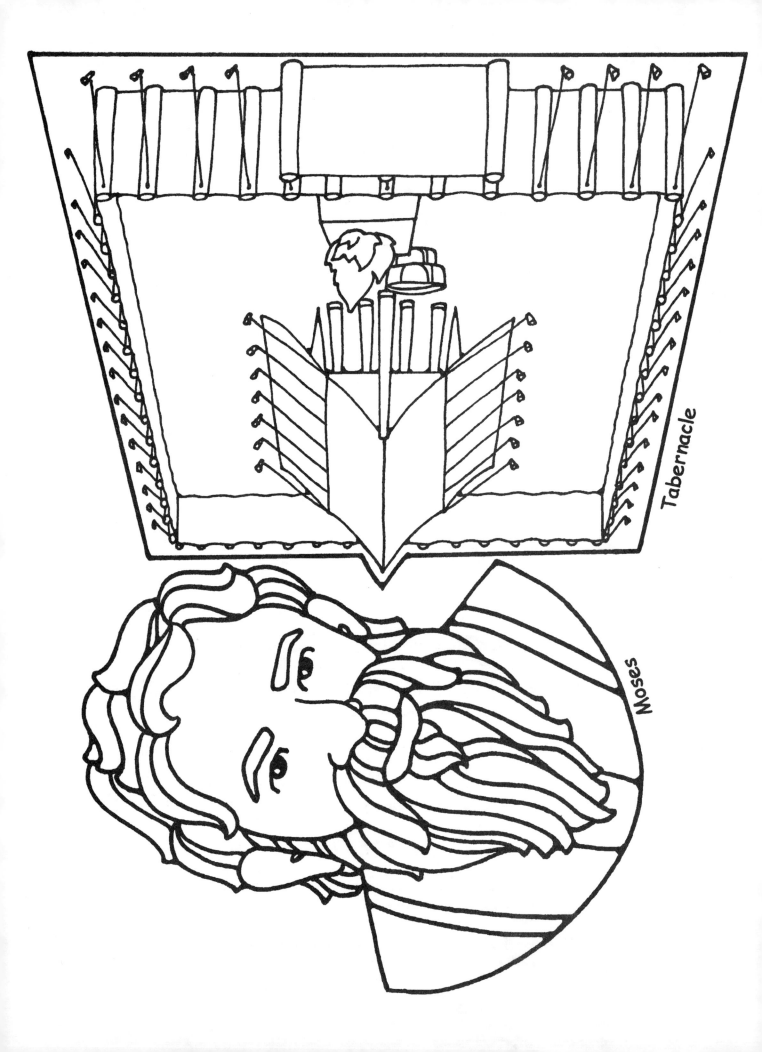

Tabernacle

Moses

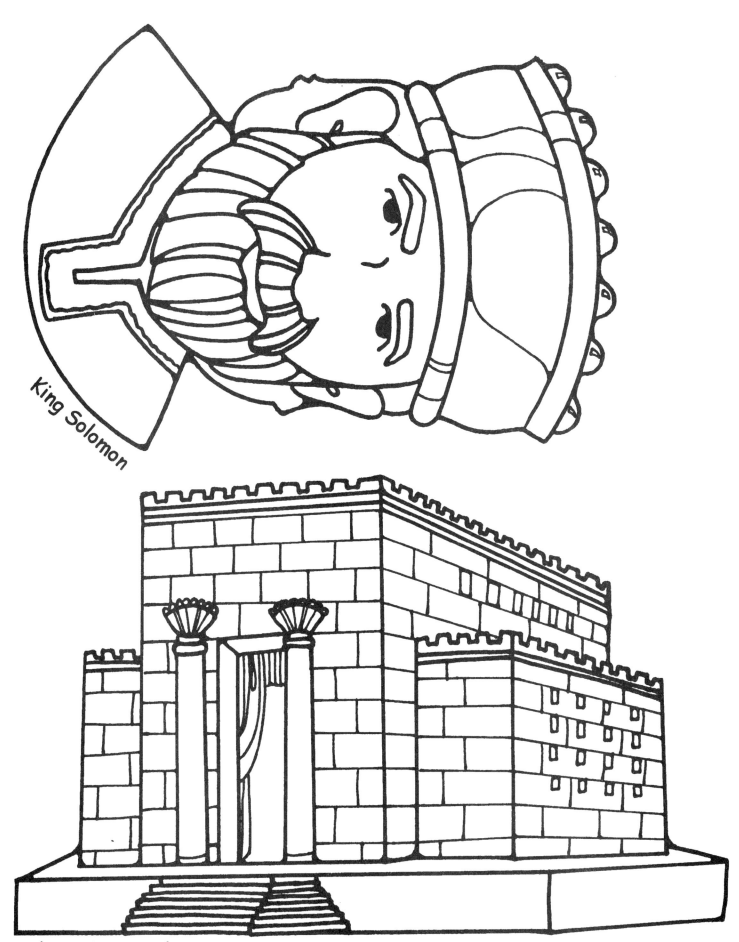

King Solomon

Solomon's Temple

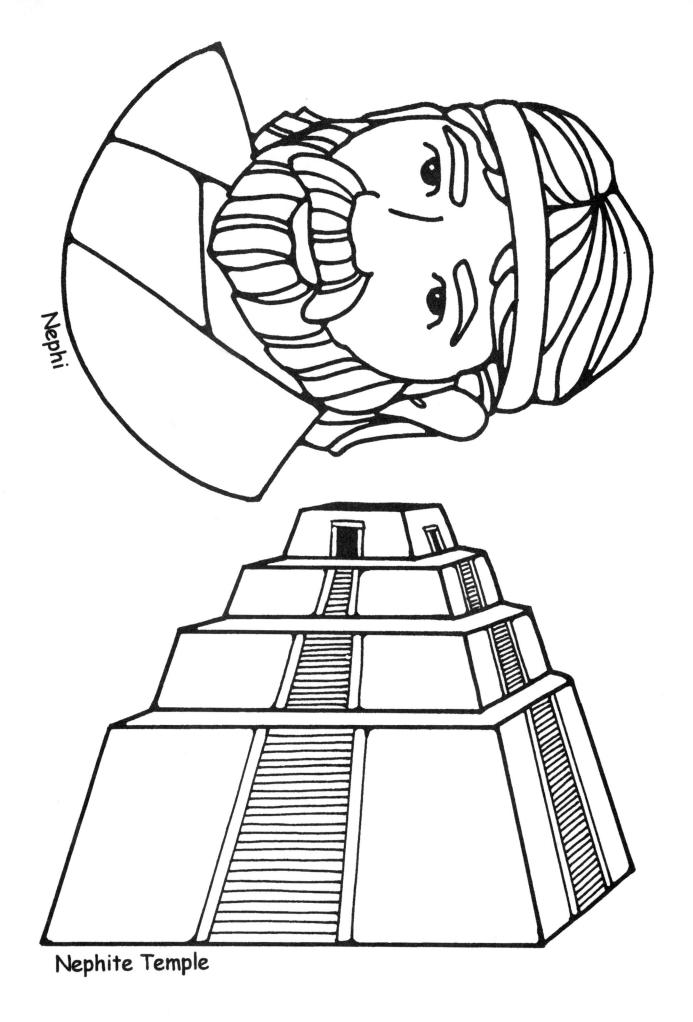

Nephi

Nephite Temple

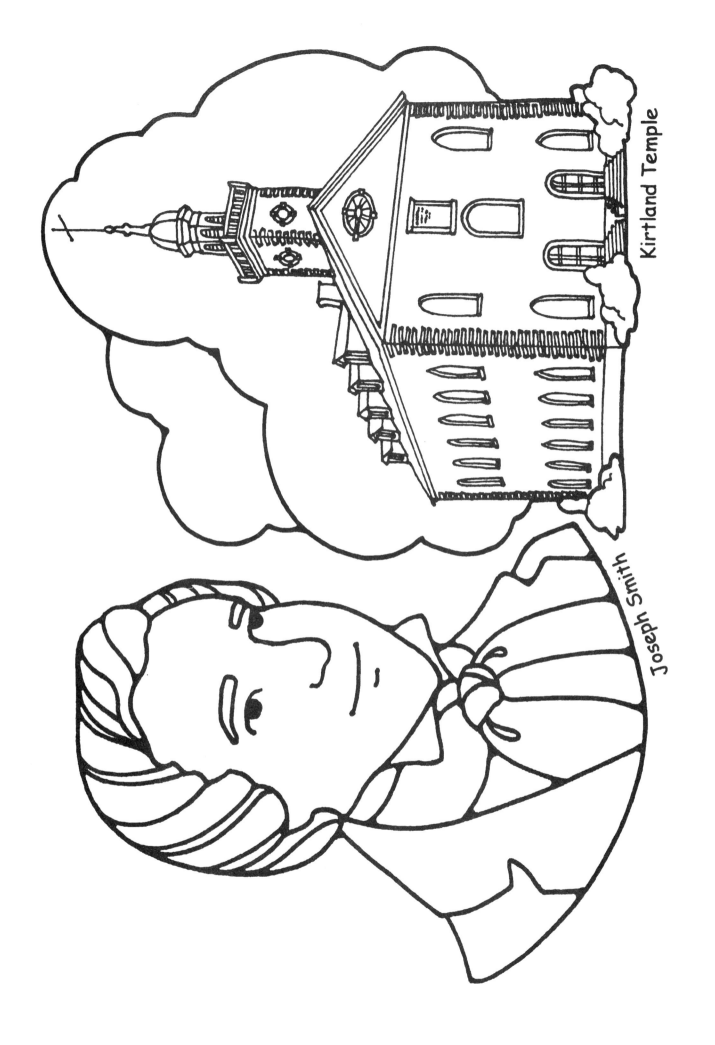

Kirtland Temple

Joseph Smith

MOSES AND THE TABERNACLE:

Moses lived in the Old Testament times. Jesus talked to Moses on Mount Sinai and said the Israelites should build a tabernacle, a place to learn about God. Jesus would come to the tabernacle. Jesus told Moses how to build the tabernacle. Jesus blessed the men so they could do the work on the tabernacle.

The Israelites obeyed Jesus, giving gold and silver for the tabernacle. They gave animal skins for the roof and beautiful cloth for the walls. The tabernacle was like a tent with a wall of curtains. An altar for sacrifice was in the yard and a gold altar in one room. A beautiful box was in the other room called the ark of the covenant. The stones with the commandments written on them were kept in the ark of the covenant.

Moses blessed the people and the tabernacle. He gave the priesthood to Aaron and his sons.

The tabernacle was a holy place, like the temple is today. Jesus placed a cloud above the tabernacle in the day and a fire above the tabernacle at night to show that Jesus was there. When the cloud moved, the Israelites took down the tabernacle and carried it with them into the wilderness.   - Exodus 24, 25, 35-39, 40, 42-43

SOLOMON AND THE TEMPLE:

King Solomon lived in Old Testament times. He was the king of Israel. He loved God and asked him to help him be a good king. Solomon told God he wanted to be wise. God told Solomon that if he obeyed God's commandments he would be wise. Solomon became the wisest man on earth, so wise that both kings and queens and people from other lands came to ask him questions.

God asked King Solomon to build a temple in Jerusalem. The temple would be the house of God. The people would not need a tabernacle anymore because they would have the temple. It would contain the ark of the covenant, a box which contained the ten commandments.

Thousands of people built the temple out of stone and the best wood from far away. The temple was beautiful. The walls and floors were covered with gold and curtains made of beautiful cloth. Gold candlesticks lighted the rooms. There was a golden altar. One room had a pool filled with water with twelve brass oxen around it.

The priests of Israel came to the temple, sang songs and thanked God for the temple. The cloud that had been over the tabernacle now filled the temple. God told the people to be righteous and they would be blessed forever.

- 1 Kings 2-10, 2 Chronicles 5-7

NEPHI (grandson of Helaman) and the Temple:

Nephi, the son of Helaman, gave the sacred records and scriptures to his son Nephi (3 Nephi 1-11).

Nephi was a righteous man. His people were called Nephites. Nephi wanted his people to believe in the Savior Jesus Christ and follow God.

The people who followed Nephi were blessed because they obeyed God and worked hard. After many years and signs that Jesus was coming, the people of Nephi gathered at the temple in the land Bountiful. The people were talking about the signs of Jesus Christ's death when all of a sudden they heard a voice from heaven that made their hearts burn. The voice was Heavenly Father asking the people to listen to His son Jesus Christ. Jesus came down from heaven and stood among the people.

Jesus asked them to come and felt the marks in His hands, feet, and side to know that He had died for their sins. The people knew He was the Savior. They fell at His feet and worshiped Him.

Jesus called Nephi and 11 other men to give them the priesthood power. He taught them the right way to baptize. He taught them that the people should believe in Him, repent, and keep the commandments to enter His kingdom. He taught them to pray and forgive one another. He healed the sick. He blessed the children. When it was time for Jesus to leave, the people cried because of their great love for Him.   - 3 Nephi

JOSEPH SMITH AND KIRTLAND:

In the latter days, 1832, Joseph Smith received revelation to build the first temple in modern times in Kirtland, Ohio.

The latter-day Saints sacrificed every extra penny they had to build the temple as they worked with all their might to build this holy temple. The Saints not only sacrificed to build the temple, their lives were threatened by those who hated them because they chose to worship God.

The women sewed clothing for the workmen and they also prepared much needed meals. The women sewed curtains to place inside the temple. The women gave up their pottery and kitchen glassware to crush and put into the outside stucco finish so the outside walls would glisten in the sun. This would be a beautiful building.

Heavenly Father, Jesus Christ, and angels appeared in the temple (D&C 137:1, 3). After it was dedicated the priesthood keys were restored, giving those in authority the sealing power to seal families together forever and to baptize and seal those who died without receiving these temple blessings.

Two years after the temple was dedicated, the Saints were forced to leave Kirtland. Their enemies took over the temple, so it was no longer a temple of God; it was just a building. Since that time, nearly 150 temples have been built.   - D&C 109

THEME 7: Temples Bless Heavenly Father's Children Throughout the World

SCRIPTURE TO MEMORIZE: | Micah 4:2 |

(shown right). See poster on page 51 and bite-size memorize card/handout on page 100.

LESSON: See More Teaching Tools on page 109. <u>Ask, "How do temples bless Heavenly Father's children throughout the world?"</u> Answer the question using the scriptures, Primary lessons, and other sources (below) to teach.

• The pioneers worked hard and sacrificed to build temples (D&C 97:12; 109:5; *Primary* 5, lessons 35, 44).

• Members of the Church today make sacrifices to go to the temple (*Primary* 5, lesson 25, enrichment activities, 4).

• There is a temple for my part of the world wherever I live.

• See the book *The First 100 Temples* by Chad S. Hawkins for more information on the temples featured here and others.

ACTIVITY: Temples Dot the Earth (Sharing Temple Stories Around the World)

OBJECTIVE: Help children learn stories of Heavenly Father's children who have lived throughout the world and the sacrifices made to bring a temple to their part of the world.

TO MAKE: *Copy, color, laminate, and cut out images (pages 152-159) as shown right.

TO SET UP: (1) Tape together and place world image on board. (2) Cut a 12" or 16" piece of string and tape it to the back of children around the world images. (3) Tape images on the walls around the room with the string attached.

ACTIVITY: Say the following:

1. "Heavenly Father's plan for all his children around the world is for them to attend the temple. Today many temples dot the earth (point to dots on map). We have nearly 150 temples built today with plans to build many more. When a temple is not within easy traveling distance, many people have work and save for many years to obtain enough money to be able to go to the temple. Then they come back home with no money and have to start over, saving their money again for the next time they wish to go. Now there are temples around the world, making it easier for the Saints to attend.

2. In the temple we perform ordinances such as baptism, endowment, and family sealings for those who have died. Because they have died, they don't have a physical body to do this work, so we can do it for them.

3. Temple work is a great and mighty work. Heavenly Father has asked us to build temples around the world.

4. The Saints made many sacrifices to build the first temples. One of the sacrifices we can make today is to pay our tithing to build future temples around the world."

TELL STORIES AROUND THE WORLD:

1. Have a child from each class select a child image (taped to the wall) and read the story that corresponds.

2. Then the child reading the story tapes the child image on the board next to the world, draping the string to the corresponding number to mark the place on the world map (as shown above).

*All images can be printed in full-color or black and white with the *Primary Partners Sharing Time: The Temple* CD-ROM.

And many nations come, and say, Come, let us go up 2 the of the Lord,... and he teach us of his ways, and we in his +s.

Micah 4:2

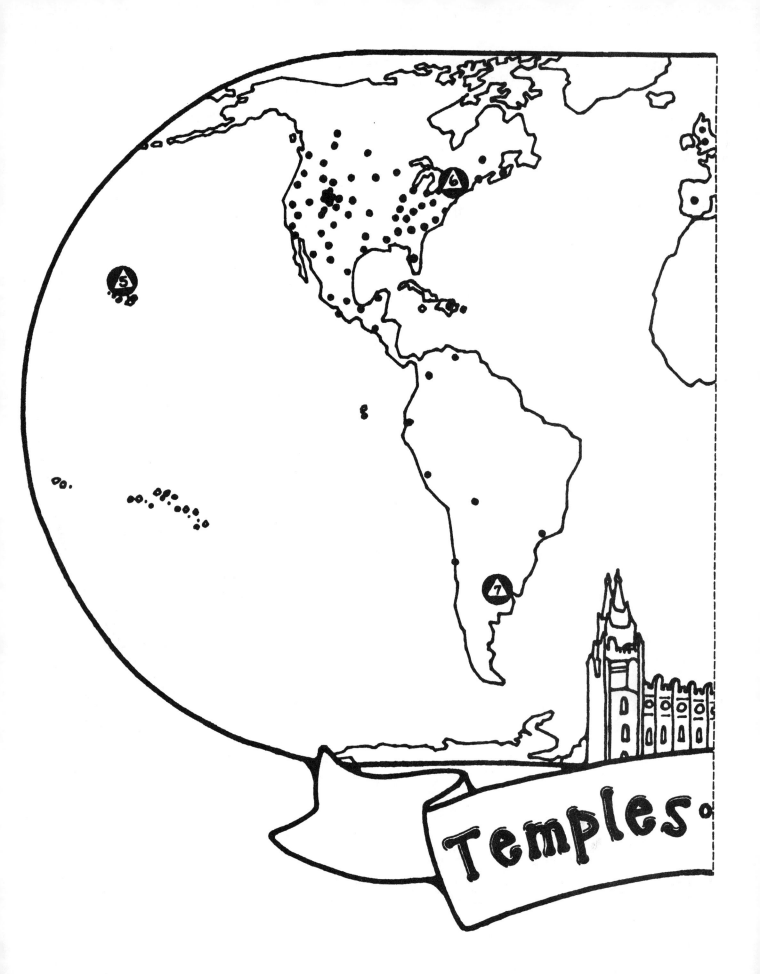

Temples

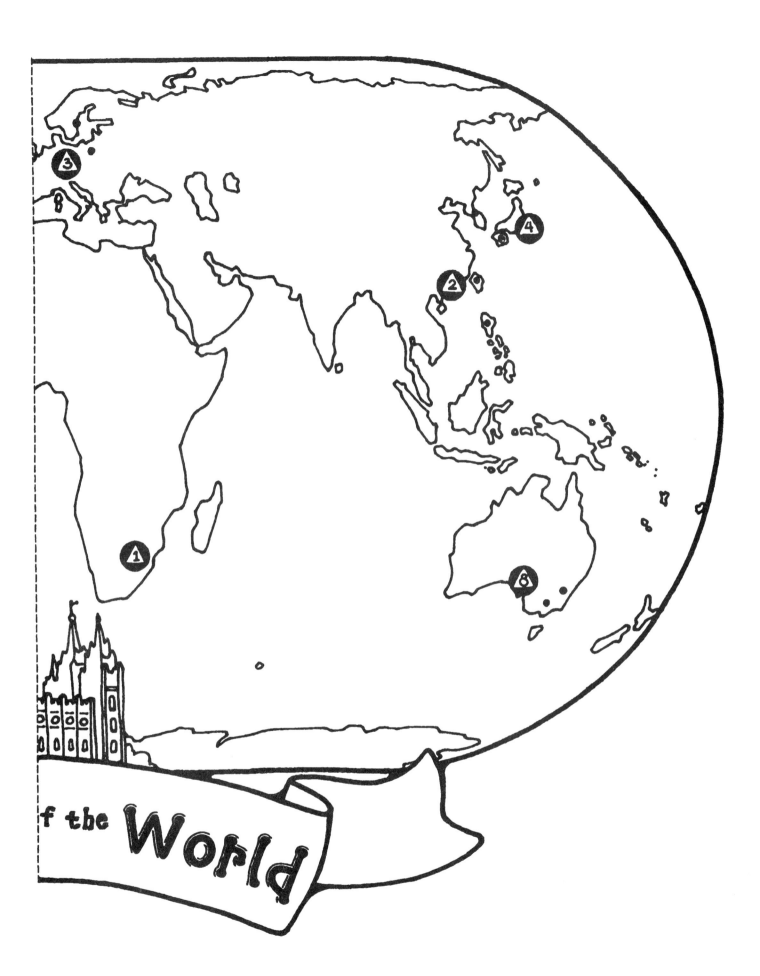

f the **World**

I am Juanita from Argentina. In 1993, I was with a group of 100 Primary children visiting the **Buenos Aires Argentina Temple**. We stood in rows of three and held hands as we slowly moved toward the temple gates. We were all dressed in white, with girls in long dresses with ribbons in our hair. The boys wore white trousers and white shirts. We each wore white shoes or covered our feet with white cloth. We carried a booklet that we made with a picture of the temple on the front. As we walked we sang, "We love to see the temple." We went into the front room of the temple. It was so beautiful. We gave prayers, testimonies, and sang. We were asked to return to the temple to be sealed to our families and receive the ordinances. The room was full of love and reverence. We kissed the temple president and his wife on the cheek as we left. When we went home we bore our testimonies to others in our ward about the importance of the temple.

I am Ruben from New York. I love to see the **Palmyra New York Temple**. Standing on the temple grounds, you can see the Sacred Grove where Joseph Smith received the vision, seeing Heavenly Father and Jesus at the age of 12. I often think of how he was my age, and how I would have felt kneeling in the grove of trees and seeing Heavenly Father and His son. The temple is built right inside the one hundred acres of Joseph Smith's family farm. The temple is so beautiful with its handcrafted stained glass windows with trees like the ones in the Sacred Grove, including 6,500 hand-made leaves. This temple is very special, because it is near the Sacred Grove where Joseph Smith saw the vision. And now, over 180 years later, the Church has spread to more than 160 nations.

I am Tembo from Africa. Before our **Johannesburg South Africa Temple** was built, people in my country had to travel to the London Temple which was eight thousand miles away. One family ate very little for a long time to save enough money to travel to the London Temple. Another family, who had five children, traveled two thousand miles to be sealed to each other in the Johannesburg South Africa Temple. Travel to the temple is still hard in Africa. The roads are few, not paved and bridges wash out. But we think our temple in Africa is a special jewel in a land famous for its diamonds. In the Johannesburg Temple, six languages are spoken, including English, Afrikaans, French, and Portuguese, so those attending can understand.

I am Megumi from Japan. The Asian Saints have waited many years to attend the **Tokyo Japan Temple**. They have had to save every penny they could to go the Hawaii Temple or New Zealand Temple, and both were very far away. Now their dreams to be sealed to their families has come true. After 70 years, Sakae Nagao, at age 89, saw her dreams come true when she was sealed to her husband in the Tokyo Japan Temple. She said, "Now I can die happy ... this is the most wonderful thing that has ever happened to me." I know that many families can be sealed, and they will be blessed because they have the temple in our part of the world.

- quotes from *The First 100 Temples*, by Chad S. Hawkins, page 58, published by Deseret Book Company, Salt Lake City, Utah.

I am Kamea from Hawaii. Aloha! This means hello and it also means good-bye. This is the way we greet those who come and go. Our **Laie Hawaii Temple** is one of great beauty with water falls leading to the front door. Our temple was promised many years after the gospel was first brought to us. Sixty-five years before the temple was built, the Hawaiian Saints were promised that if they were faithful, they would one day be sealed to their families for eternity. Building this temple was difficult as it was hard to find building material. Just when it was needed a blessing came. Within two days a bad storm left a ship stranded on the coral reef nearby. For helping the captain unload his ship, the Saints were given the lumber they needed to build our temple. Because of their faith, Heavenly Father blessed the righteous with this temple of paradise. Here thousands of missionary referrals are sent out as nonmember visitors tour the grounds and visitors center. Aloha!

I am Lambert from Germany. I live near the **Freiberg Temple**, which was built behind the Iron Curtain. This was a wall in Berlin that kept the German people on the East separated from the people on the West during World War II. Many families were separated as some went on the East side of the wall and others stayed on the West. For many years they couldn't even see or talk to each other. This was a sad time for many families. During this time the Freiberg Temple was built on the East side because the Saints there prayed for this blessing and received it. As a girl, one woman and her family went to the Freiberg Temple with a group of Ukrainian Saints. There she was sealed to her family for eternity. They traveled thousands of miles through the Communist Bloc to attend the temple. They had little money and were unable to buy things, so they had to carry their own food and

sleeping bags. Nevertheless, while they were there, they had a "wonderful feeling of heaven" and felt the "presence of the Savior" (Hawkins, *The First 100 Temples*, pages 93-94).

I'm Suling from China. One third of the entire world's population lives in China. We don't have enough land in our country so it is very valuable. Our **Hong Kong China Temple** is six stories high, because the land is so expensive. To purchase new land it may cost many millions of dollars for one tiny piece of land. President Hinckley was discouraged at the high cost of land. One night he woke up with the idea to build the temple on the site of the mission home and chapel that was already there. The temple was built and now the mission home is part of the temple. Before the temple was dedicated, thirteen thousand people came to see this temple. The people noticed a feeling of peace and reverence here, even though it is very noisy outside in this city full of people with the cars and noise of

city life all around. I love to be near this temple as it gives the people of China a chance to be sealed to their families forever!

I am Niles from Australia. I live near the **Adelaide Australia Temple**. We are blessed to have to have more than one temple in Australia. The Church of Jesus Christ of Latter-day Saints is the fastest growing church in Australia. When our temple was dedicated, my friends and I were able to miss school and attend. My parents have gone to this temple. They say they have warm feelings when they go into the baptismal area and in the sealing room. Soon our family will go to the temple to be sealed together for eternity. I can't wait to go, because I know that this will bring our family happiness and peace, knowing we can be together forever.

THEME #8: We Serve Others Through Temple Work

SCRIPTURE TO MEMORIZE: Malachi 4:6

(shown right). See poster on page 61 and bite-size memorize card/handout on page 100.

LESSON: See More Teaching Tools on page 109. <u>Ask, "How can we serve others through temple work?"</u> Answer the question using the scriptures, Primary lessons, and other sources (below) to teach.

• In the temple, ordinances are performed for our families and others who have died without receiving ordinances such as baptism, endowments, and sealings (D&C 138:53-58; *Primary* 5, lesson 34).

• I can prepare to serve in the temple by learning about my ancestors and doing family history work (D&C 138:47-48; *Gospel Principles*, chapter 40; *Family Home Evening Resource Book*, lesson ideas, "Genealogy").

• I can write my personal history and write in my journal (1 Nephi 9; 19:1; *Family Home Evening Resource Book*, lesson ideas, "Journals").

ACTIVITY: Turning the Hearts of the Children to the Fathers

(Finding Temple Workers Concentration Game)

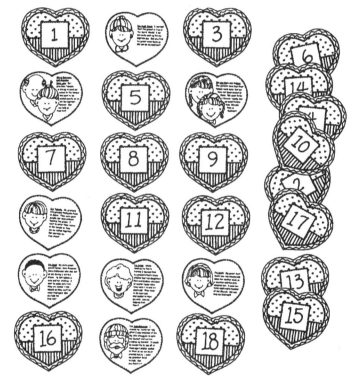

OBJECTIVE: Help children match the temple workers to those who are waiting for their temple work to be done. Inspire children to do temple work for their departed dead.

TO MAKE:

1. *Copy the hearts (page 62) six times. Color and cut out. Write a number (1-18) in the square of each heart (shown right).

2. *Copy, color, and cut out the heart cards with faces (pages 63-68).

3. Laminate all cards for durability.

4. Place double-stick tape on the back of each face heart and tape to a poster or the board randomly.

5. Tape the numbered heart over each face heart by placing two pieces of tape at the top to lift the heart up and down when the number is guessed.

FOR JUNIOR PRIMARY: Cut the number of matches in half and choose the ones they can easily understand.

ACTIVITY: Tell children that there are temple ordinances such as baptisms, endowments, and sealings that need to be performed for people who were not baptized or sealed to their families before they died. We can prepare to serve in the temple by learning about our ancestors and doing family history work. We can read personal family histories to learn of our ancestors and records to learn if this important work has been done. Let's learn about some girls and boys who are helping their ancestors, and about these ancestors who are waiting to have this important temple work done.

• With images on the board set up (see #4 and 5 above), have children take turns turning two cards over to make a match.

WAYS TO PLAY: You could divide into teams and take turns playing, or toss a bean bag over your shoulder to choose the next player. You could still play in teams, just toss the beanbag to the next team playing to choose a new player. Option: Instead of a beanbag you could toss a soft ball or bean bag toy.

• To make a match, pay attention to the names, e.g., Kayla, who is doing the temple work for Aunt Sadie, will match up with Aunt Sadie, who is looking for Kayla to do her baptismal work.

*All images can be printed in full-color with the *Primary Partners Sharing Time: The Temple* CD-ROM.

Malachi 4:6

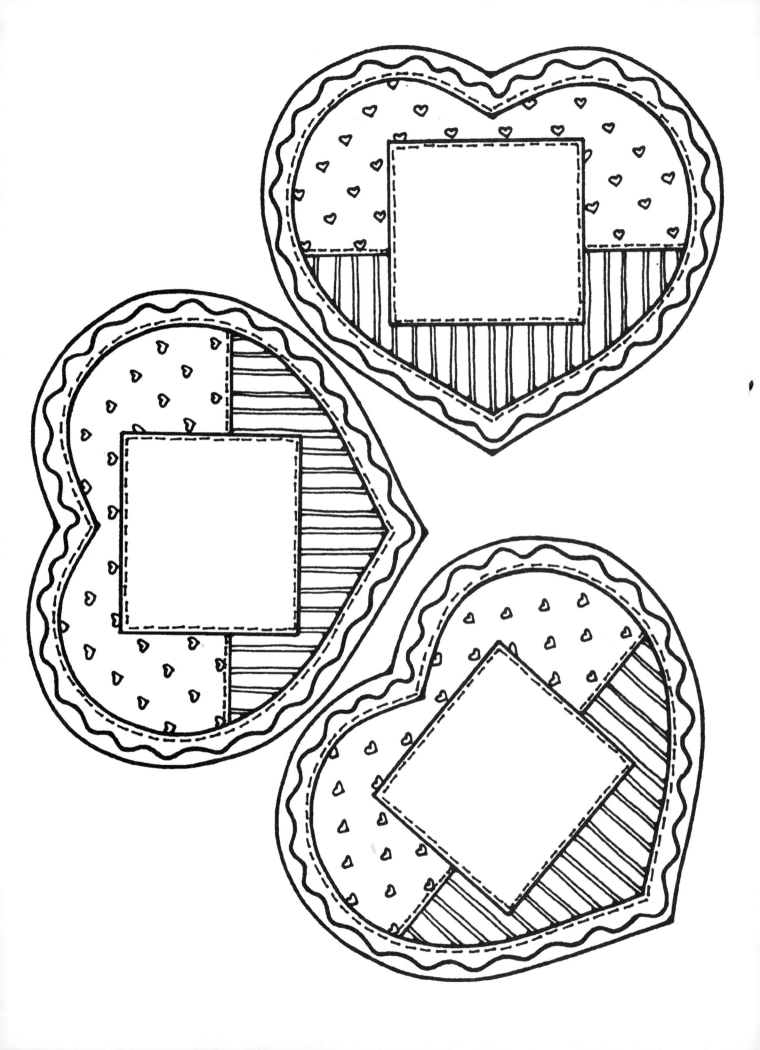

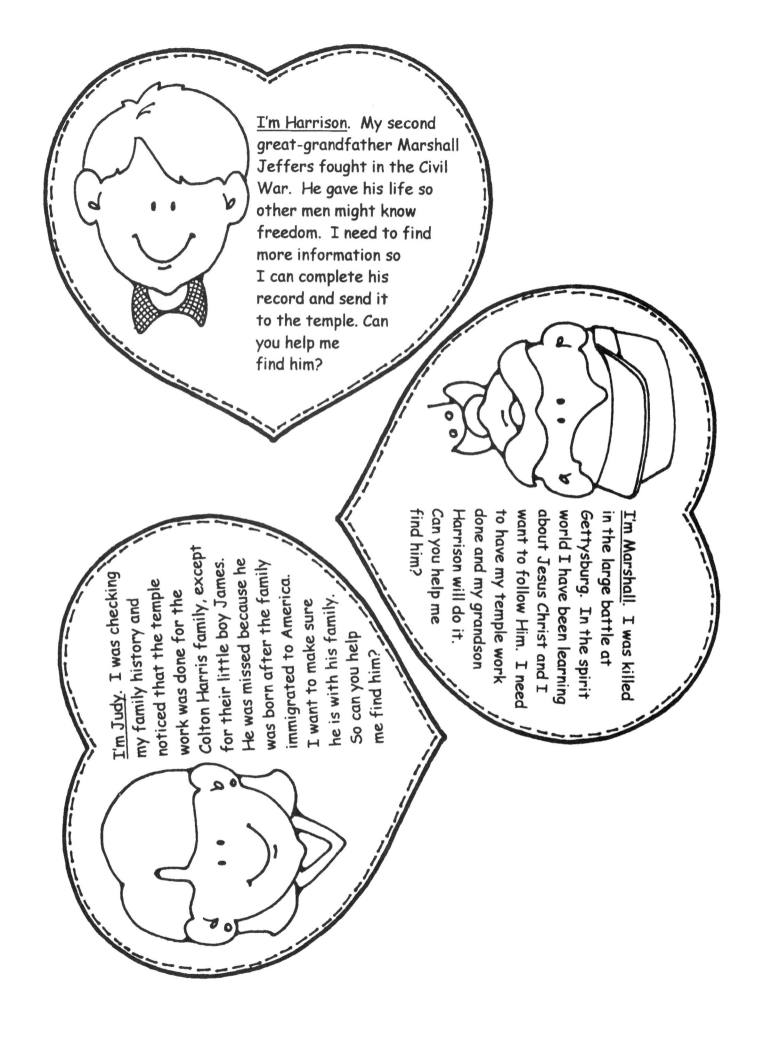

I'm Harrison. My second great-grandfather Marshall Jeffers fought in the Civil War. He gave his life so other men might know freedom. I need to find more information so I can complete his record and send it to the temple. Can you help me find him?

I'm Marshall. I was killed in the large battle at Gettysburg. In the spirit world I have been learning about Jesus Christ and I want to follow Him. I need to have my temple work done and my grandson Harrison will do it. Can you help me find him?

I'm Judy. I was checking my family history and noticed that the temple work was done for the Colton Harris family, except for their little boy James. He was missed because he was born after the family immigrated to America. I want to make sure he is with his family. So can you help me find him?

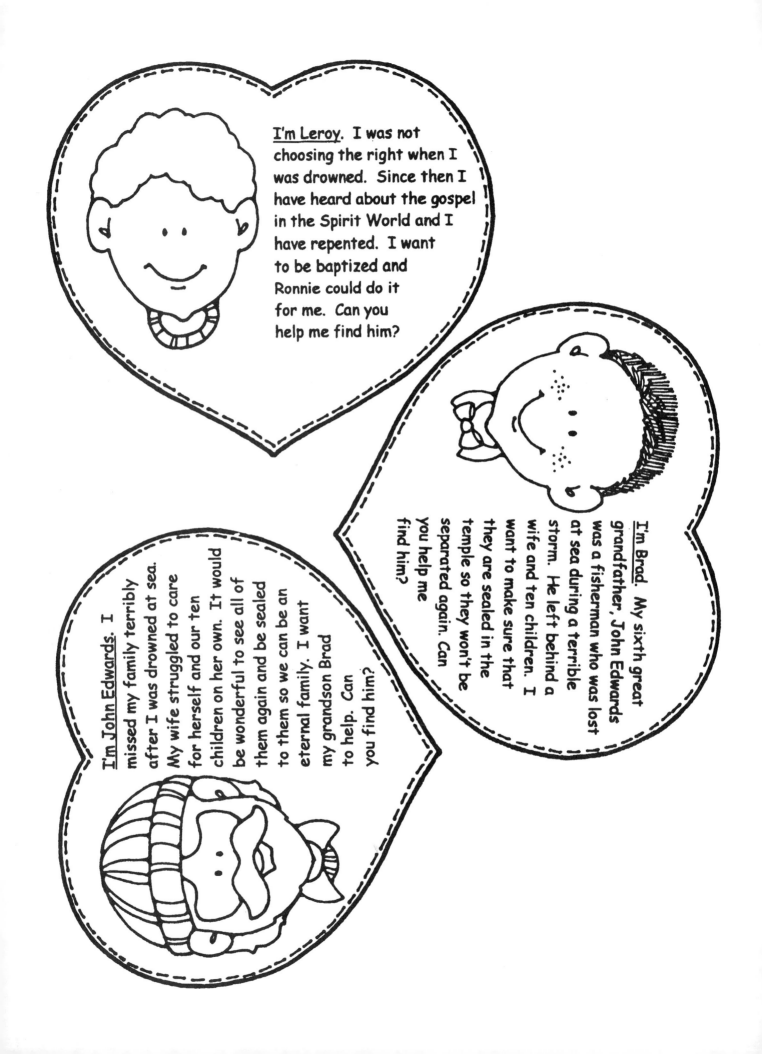

I'm Leroy. I was not choosing the right when I was drowned. Since then I have heard about the gospel in the Spirit World and I have repented. I want to be baptized and Ronnie could do it for me. Can you help me find him?

I'm Brad. My sixth great grandfather, John Edwards was a fisherman who was lost at sea during a terrible storm. He left behind a wife and ten children. I want to make sure that they are sealed in the temple so they won't be separated again. Can you help me find him?

I'm John Edwards. I missed my family terribly after I was drowned at sea. My wife struggled to care for herself and our ten children on her own. It would be wonderful to see all of them again and be sealed to them so we can be an eternal family. I want my grandson Brad to help. Can you find him?

I'm Jenny. My friend Amanda was killed in a car crash when she was nine years old. She was not a member of the Church and I want to be baptized for her in the temple. So can you help me find her?

I'm Amanda. My friend Jenny told me about Jesus Christ. I wanted to be baptized, but didn't have a chance as I was killed in a car crash. Since I only have a spirit body now I can't be baptized, so would you find Jenny for me so she can be baptized for me?

I'm Ronnie. My Uncle Leroy was a rebellious boy when he drowned in a river near our home. If he had lived longer, he might have accepted the gospel and been baptized. I hope that he would like me to be baptized for him, so will you help me find him?

We are Fern and Colleen. Our parents have had their temple work done, but we have not been sealed to them. We want to be a forever family, but we need Emily's help. Can you help us find her?

I'm Emily. While reading my family history I learned that my grandmother's Uncle Clayton had two daughters, Fern and Colleen who died of scarlet fever when they were five and six years old. They need to be baptized and sealed to their parents. Can you help me find them?

We're Grandma and Grandpa Nishijima. Our grandson Takashi is trying to send our names to the temple. We want to be sealed quickly so we can be together forever. Can you help us find him?

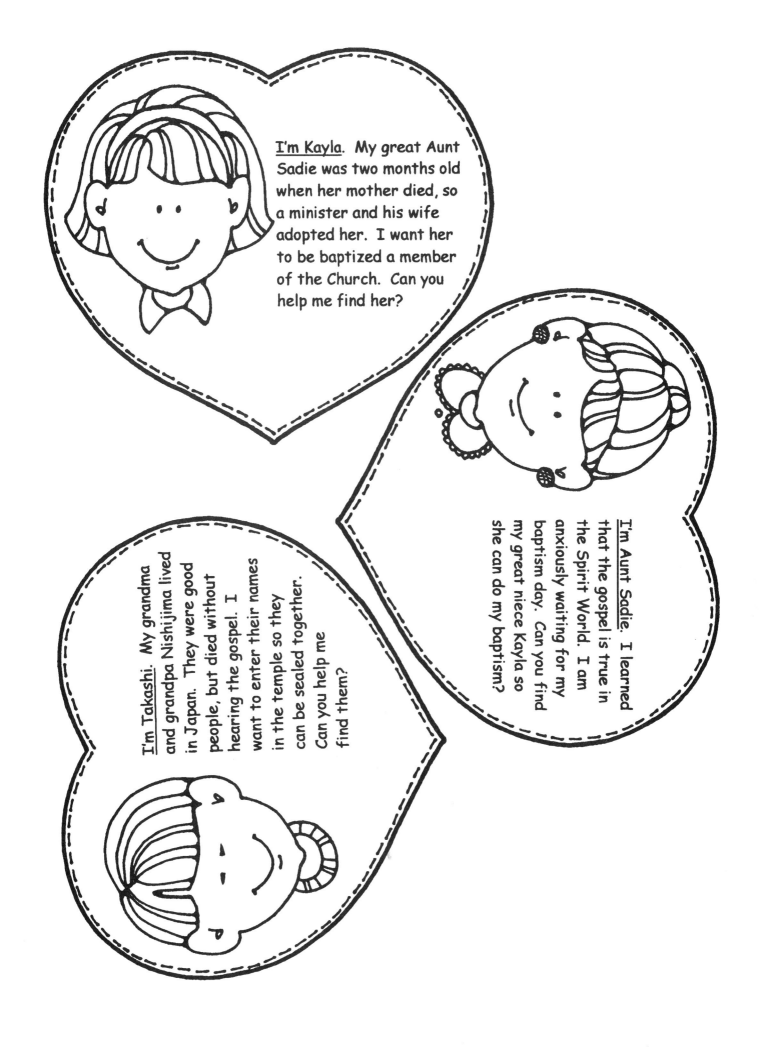

I'm Kayla. My great Aunt Sadie was two months old when her mother died, so a minister and his wife adopted her. I want her to be baptized a member of the Church. Can you help me find her?

I'm Aunt Sadie. I learned that the gospel is true in the Spirit World. I am anxiously waiting for my baptism day. Can you find my great niece Kayla so she can do my baptism?

I'm Takashi. My grandma and grandpa Nishijima lived in Japan. They were good people, but died without hearing the gospel. I want to enter their names in the temple so they can be sealed together. Can you help me find them?

I'm James. I have been waiting to join my family for a very long time. All of their work has been done, but my name was not on the record in England, so I was not included in the family sealing. I have a relative named Judy that does her family history and hope she will find the mistake. Can you help me find her?

I'm Stella. My great-grandmother Ethel Petersen wrote in her journal about the roses she planted outside her home in Denmark. She was 93 when she heard the gospel. She wanted to be baptized but died before she had the chance. I want to make sure she is baptized. Can you help me find her?

I'm Ethel Petersen. My great granddaughter Stella cared enough to read my journal and find out that I died before I was baptized. I enjoyed my lovely rose garden, but I didn't have the chance to enjoy the beauty of the gospel. Will you help me find her so she can be baptized for me?

THEME #9: I Will Live Now to Be Worthy to Go to the Temple and Serve a Mission

SCRIPTURE TO MEMORIZE: | John 14:21 |

(shown right). See poster on page 70 and bite-size memorize card/handout on page 101.

LESSON: See More Teaching Tools on pages 110-111. <u>Ask, "How can we live now to be worthy to go to the temple and serve a mission?"</u> Answer the question using the scriptures, Primary lessons, and other sources (below) to teach.

• I will pay my tithing (*Primary* 3, lesson 42, *Primary* 7, lesson 24).
• I will be honest with Heavenly Father, others, and myself (*Primary* 2, lesson 34; *Primary* 6, lesson 14).
• I will do those things on the Sabbath that will help me feel close to Heavenly Father (*Primary* 2, lesson 37; *Primary* 7, lesson 14).
• I will seek good friends and treat others kindly (*Primary* 1, less. 33; *Primary* 7, less. 20).
• I will share the gospel with others (*Primary* 3, lesson 25; *Primary* 4, lesson 17).

ACTIVITY: Traveling Toward the Temple and a Mission
(Wrong or Worthy Choices Car puzzles)

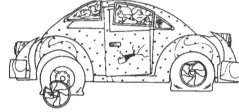

OBJECTIVE: Help children make choices by putting together two different puzzles that represent wrong and right choices that will help them to be worthy to go to the temple or serve a mission.

TO MAKE: (1) *Copy, color, and cut out two cars and one set of car parts, plus wordstrips (pages 71-76). (2) Glue-mount the BC (Bad Choice) wordstrips on the back of the wrecked/broken down car parts and the GC (Good Choice) wordstrips on the back of the good car parts. (3) Set up the two car puzzles on two posters or on the board with double-stick tape, as shown above.

ACTIVITY: Tell children, "If we are to be worthy to go to the temple, and/or serve a mission, we need to make worthy choices. Bad choices keep us away from the temple and serving a mission, and good choices help us to be worthy to enter the temple and serve a mission."

1. Point to the broken down car on the left and the good working car on the right.
2. Tell children, "(1) Think of yourself as a car that needs working parts if it is to travel down the road. With this activity we will build two different cars: one that is wrecked and broken down, and one that has good working parts (point to the car on the right). (2) With a broken windshield, you can't see. With a flat tire, the car won't travel very far. With a dented fender and broken headlight, you wouldn't be able to see where you are going at night. Each day we make choices that determine how our car will run. If you make a bad choice you can fix it by repenting and not repeating the wrong choice. You can replace a flat with a good tire, a broken window with a good window, a dented fender and broken headlight with a good fender with a working light. (3) To make life easy, we need to make good choices every day so we don't have to keep stopping and repairing our car. Heavenly Father wants us to be worthy to go to the temple and to serve a mission when the time comes, so let's keep our car in good working order by making good choices each day."
3. Take the parts off the poster/board and mix up in a container (removing tape first). Have children take turns drawing a puzzle piece and reading it. The BC (Bad Choice) parts should be placed on the left to make a broken down or wrecked car. The GC (Good Choice) parts should be placed on the right to make a good car.

*All images can be printed in full-color with the *Primary Partners Sharing Time: The Temple* CD-ROM.

He t+ hath my , and peth them, he it is t+ eth me.

John 14:21

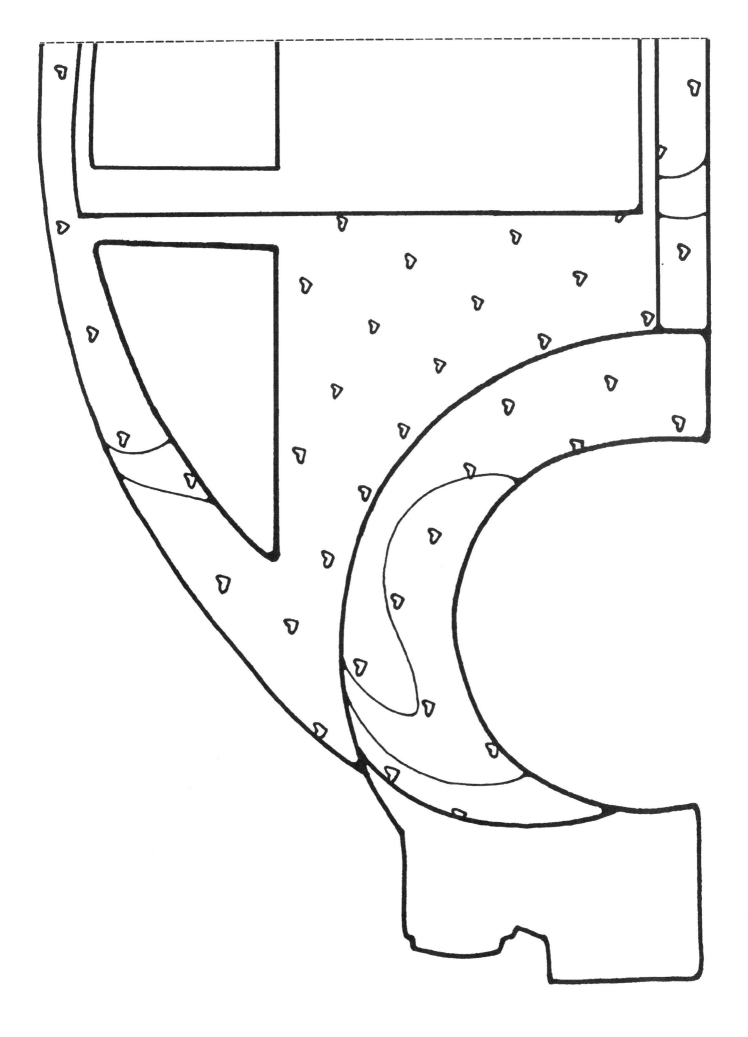

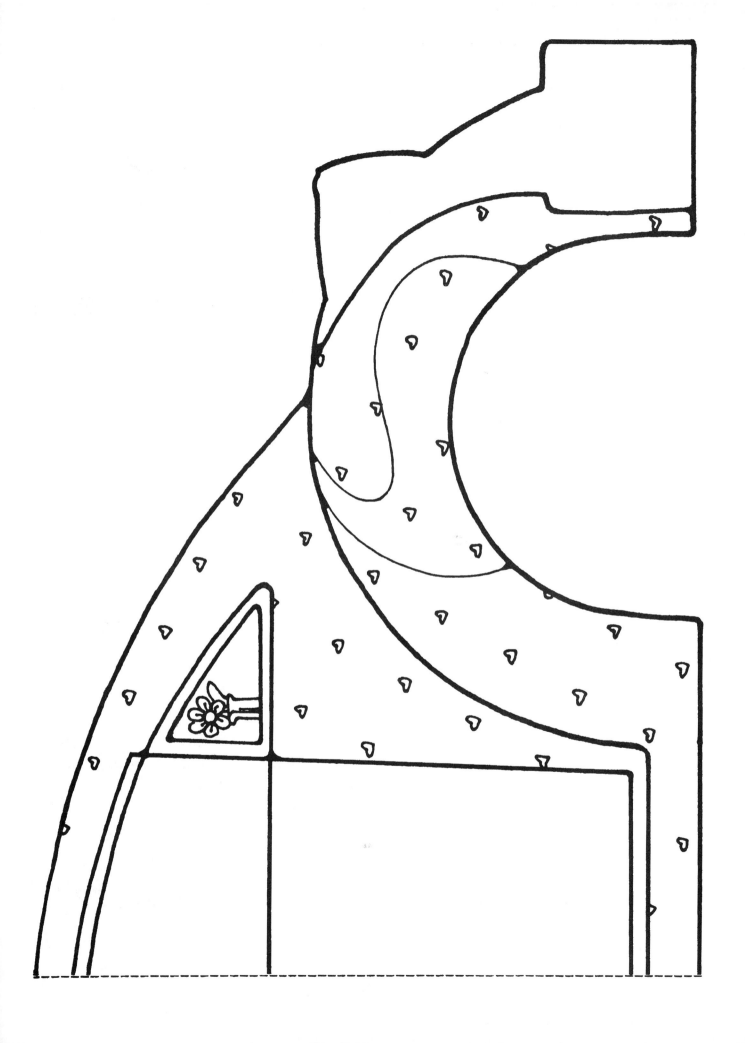

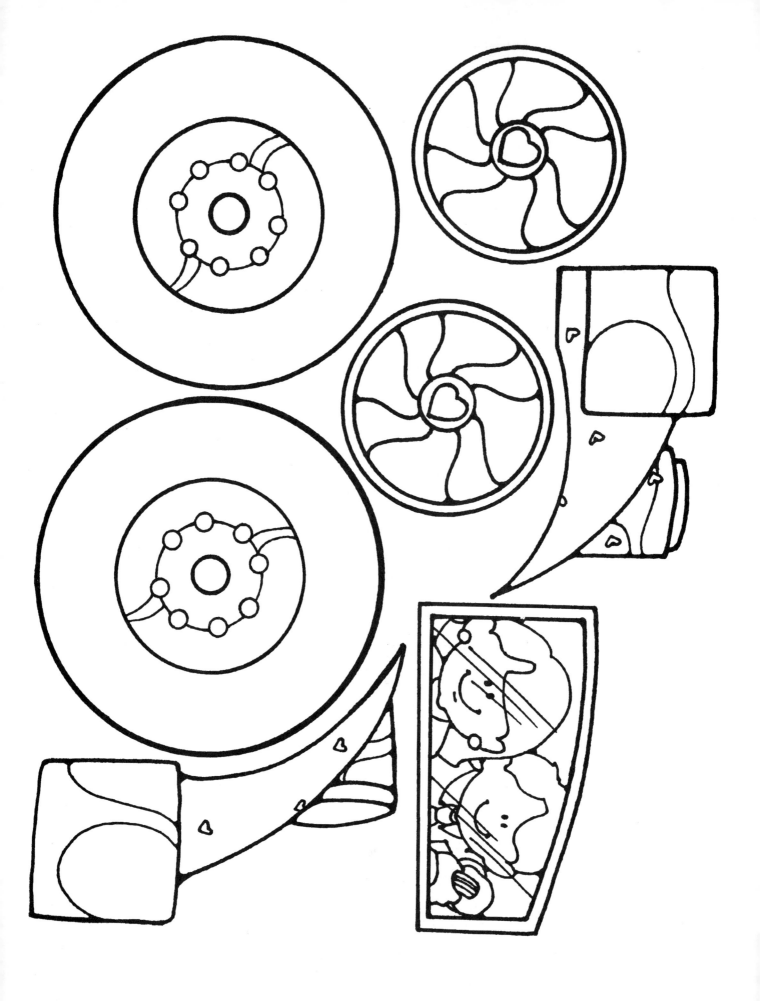

BAD CHOICES to glue on the back of wrecked/broken car parts:	GOOD CHOICES to glue on the back of good car parts:

BC: I went shopping on Sunday, so I didn't keep the Sabbath day holy.

GC: I want to go to the temple someday, so I told the truth.

BC: I was asked to smoke a cigarette, so I did.

GC: I earned some money and paid my tithing so I could help build temples.

BC: I thought it was okay to take some drugs. They were free.

GC: I like to share my toys, so I donate the toys I don't use to the poor.

BC: I decided not to go to church because I was too tired to get out of bed.

GC: When mother asks me to do something, I obey.

BC: I thought it was okay to swear because my friend did.

GC: I am reverent when I am in Heavenly Father's house.

BC: I watched a TV show my mother said I shouldn't watch.

GC: I pray morning, noon, and night to keep heaven in sight.

BC: I heard gossip about someone. I didn't know if it was true or not, but I told my friends anyway.

GC: I am kind to others, even when they are not kind to me.

BC: I told mother I would watch my sister, but I left her alone when my friend asked me to play at his house.

GC: I am honest by not taking things that don't belong to me.

BC: I had a chance to help my neighbor, but I went for a bike ride instead.

GC: When someone asks me to take drugs, I said "no."

THEME #10: I Prepare to Go to the Temple as I Follow Heavenly Father's Plan for Me

SCRIPTURE TO MEMORIZE: | Articles of Faith 1:4 |

(shown right). See poster on page 78 and bite-size memorize card/handout on page 101.

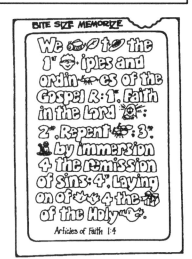

BITE SIZE MEMORIZE

We ♡ ♪ to the 1" 👄 iples and ordin-☞es of the Gospel R: 1". Faith in the Lord 👁: 2". Repent 🐟: 3". 👤 by immersion 4 the remission of sins: 4". Laying on of 👐 4 the 🎁 of the Holy 👻.

Articles of Faith 1:4

LESSON: See More Teaching Tools on pages 112-114. <u>Ask, "How do we prepare to go to the temple?"</u> Answer the question using the scriptures, Primary lessons, and other sources (below) to teach.

• I have faith in the Lord Jesus Christ. I will remember my baptismal covenants and listen to the Holy Ghost. See Alma 37:33; *Primary* 6, lesson 6; 1999 and 2000 *Outline for Sharing Time and the Children's Sacrament Meeting Presentation.*

• I will choose the right. I know I can repent when I make a mistake (*Primary* 3, lesson 2, 10).

• My testimony will grow as I study the scriptures, pray, go to Church, and follow the prophet (2 Nephi 31:14-21; 32:8-9; *Primary* 5, lesson 46).

ACTIVITY: Choices to Prepare for the Temple (No Worms in My Apple testimony tree)

OBJECTIVE: Help children think of ways they can strengthen their testimony, follow Heavenly Father's plan and prepare to go to the temple.

TO MAKE:

1. *Copy, color, and cut out tree parts and apples (pages 78-84).
2. Glue-mount tree on a poster and laminate for durability.
3. Place apples in a container and have double-stick tape ready to place apples on the tree or below the tree.

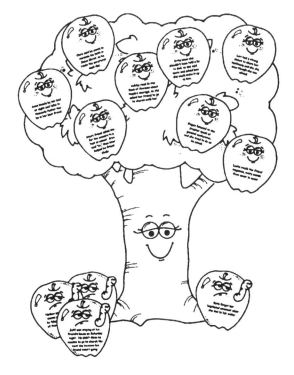

ACTIVITY:

1. Post the tree on the board and two apples, a good and a bad. Place the good apple in the tree and the wormy or bad apple on the ground and say, "We can prepare to go to the temple as we follow Heavenly Father's plan and do things each day that strengthen rather than weaken our testimony. An apple growing in a tree is a good apple until it gets a worm in it. Let's think of the worm as a bad choice. Once the worm gets into the apple, it eats away at the apple, destroying the fruit. In our life we need to keep the worms out of our apple so that we can be strong. A strong testimony is like a good apple that comes from good choices."

2. Take the good and the wormy apple from the tree and place it in a container with the rest of the apples.

3. Have children take turns drawing apples from the container and reading them aloud. Have children place them in the tree if it is a good choice apple and on the ground if it is a bad choice apple.

4. Tell children that when apples are harvested and placed in a box or basket they will stay fresh, unless one apple goes bad. When one apple goes bad and begins to rot, it makes the other apples start to rot. Let's all be good apples and have strong testimony so we are a positive influence, rather than a "rotten" influence on our friends. We need to have a strong testimony so that we can be a good example for our friends. This way they too can prepare to go to the temple and share the blessings Heavenly Father has for us all.

*All images can be printed in full-color with the *Primary Partners Sharing Time: The Temple* CD-ROM.

BITE SIZE MEMORIZE

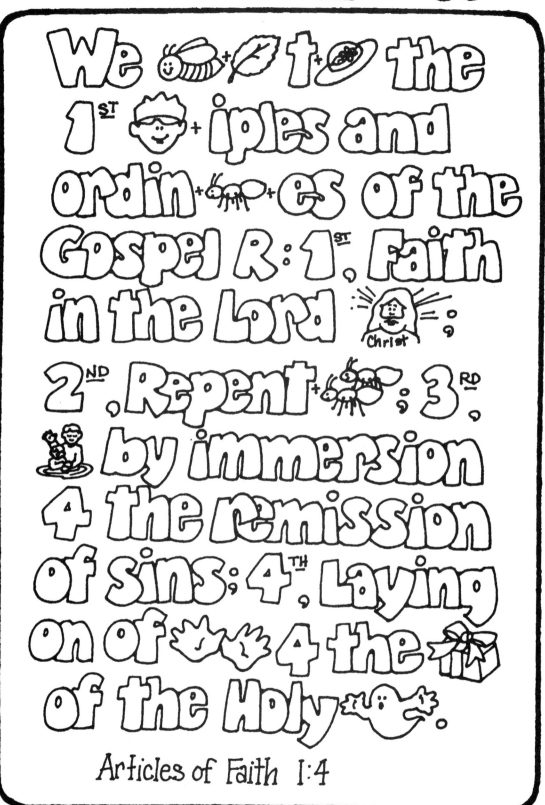

We believe to the 1st principles and ordinances of the Gospel R: 1st, Faith in the Lord Christ 2nd, Repentance; 3rd, Baptism by immersion 4 the remission of sins; 4th, Laying on of hands 4 the gift of the Holy Ghost.

Articles of Faith 1:4

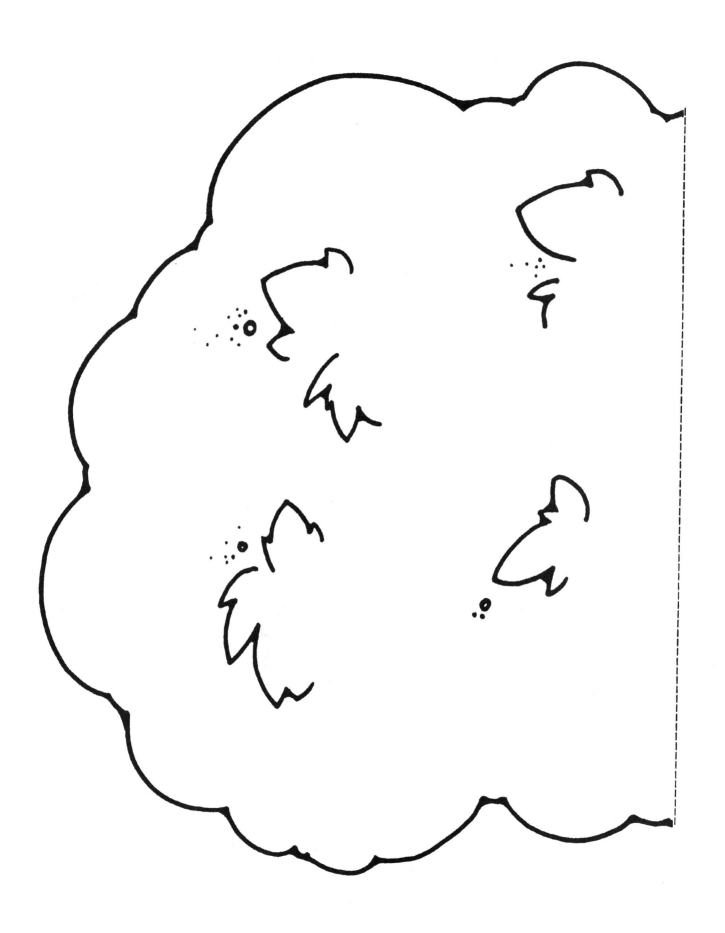

Anna kneels by her bed at night and talks to Heavenly Father like he is her best friend.

Jason knew it was time for scripture study, but he turned on the TV instead.

Lori had a strong desire to share her testimony and she did, even though she was afraid.

Nathan saw some gummy worms at the store, so he filled his pockets full of them without paying.

Chris said he wants to increase his faith in Jesus Christ, so he reads the scriptures each day.

Leslie reads the *Friend* magazine, every month from cover to cover.

Erika knew she shouldn't have told a lie to her dad, so she said sorry and asked how she could make it up to him.

Beth forgot her baptismal covenant when she lied to her sister.

Ashley read in the Book of Mormon about Nephi's courage, so she asked her friend to go to church with her.

Jeff was staying at his friend's house on Saturday night. He didn't think he needed to go to church the next day because his friend wasn't going.

Megan listened to the prophet speak at general conference, and she tried to do as he asked.

Stan's friend asked him for the answers to a test at school. Stan said "no," then later helped his friend study.

Sarah noticed that a girl at school didn't have any friends, so Sarah went over to talk to her.

Abby saw that her mother was tired, so she offered to do the dishes.

Chad didn't listen to the Holy Ghost when he felt an impression to get off the trampoline. He kept jumping, fell off and broke his leg.

When it comes time for family prayer, Jenny is always there.

Caroline knew she should not smoke, but tried a cigarette anyway.

Tim was tempted to spend his tithing money on a new baseball, but he paid it instead.

THEME #11: I Am Thankful for Temple Blessings

SCRIPTURE TO MEMORIZE: D&C 110:6

(shown right). See poster on page 86 and bite-size memorize card/handout on page 115.

LESSON: See More Teaching Tools on page 101. Ask, "How does the temple bless us?"
Answer question using the scriptures, Primary lessons, and sources (below) to teach.
• I am thankful to know that Heavenly Father has a plan for my family to be together
(D&C 59:23; *LDS Temples*, 74-75; *Primary 3*, lesson 35, enrichment activity 1).
• Temple blessings help me feel happiness and peace in my life and in my home
(*Primary* 2, lesson 1; *Primary 4*, lesson 38).
• Temple blessings help me know that Heavenly Father and Jesus Christ
love me. I can show my gratitude to them (D&C 78:18-19; *Primary* 2, lesson 24).

ACTIVITY:
Celestial Blessings
(Sunshine Show-and-tell)

OBJECTIVE: Help children realize
blessings that come from temple
ordinances.

TO MAKE:
1. *Copy, color, and cut out Celestial
Blessing sun, temple, and sunshine
show-and-tell sun rays (pages 87-92).
2. Mount Celestial Blessings sun and
temple on a poster or board.
3. Place rays around the room on the
walls or under chairs with double-stick
tape.

ACTIVITY: Tell children that we can
obtain the blessings of the celestial
kingdom if we are worthy. The celestial
kingdom is where Heavenly Father and
Jesus live. Everyone will be resurrected
and live forever with a resurrected body,
but not everyone will have eternal life.
Eternal life is life with Heavenly Father

and Jesus in the celestial kingdom. We can obtain these celestial blessings by living the commandments and participating in
temple ordinances that are necessary for us to enter into the celestial kingdom. The temple ordinances of baptism,
endowment, and eternal marriage are available to us. All we have to do is follow Heavenly Father's plan and we can have
these celestial blessings. Let's spread a little sunshine each day by reminding ourselves and our families of these celestial
blessings.
1. Have children look around the room for the sun rays.
2. Take turns drawing a sun ray and reading it aloud. Complete the sentence after the word "because ..." explaining why
the temple ordinances are a blessing. For example, "My ancestors can also enjoy the blessings of the temple because
I can have their families sealed together forever."

*All images can be printed in full-color or black and white with the *Primary Partners Sharing Time: The Temple* CD-ROM.

Let the ♥ of all my 👦👧👦 rejoice, 🦉 who have ... built this 🏠 2 my name.

D&C 110:6

If a member of my family dies, I can feel peace because. . .

When I see the temple, I feel Heavenly Father's love because. . .

I am grateful that I can be married in the temple because...

I am happy to know that Heavenly Father has great blessings waiting for me because...

My ancestors can also enjoy the blessings of the temple because. . . .

I want to love and serve my family here on earth because. . . .

The priesthood ordinances performed in the temple are important because...

The temple helps me to be with Heavenly Father and Jesus again because...

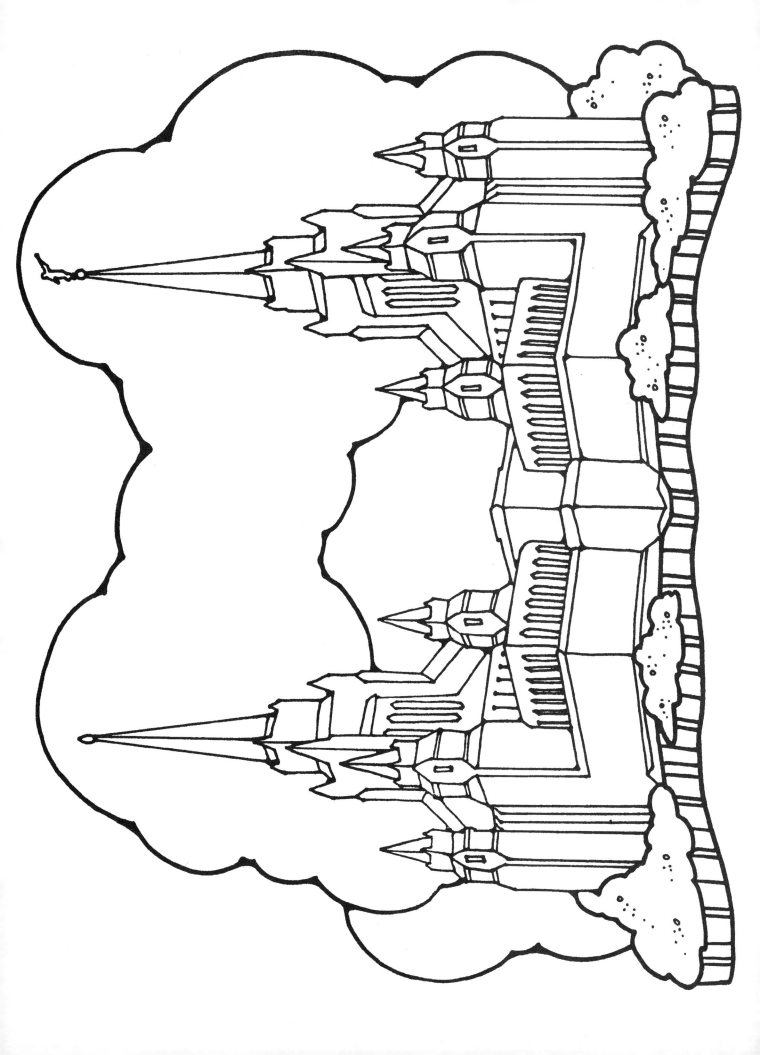

THEME #12: When Jesus Comes Again, He Will Come to the Temple

SCRIPTURE TO MEMORIZE: | D&C 34:11-12 |

(shown right). See poster on page 94 and bite-size memorize card/handout on p. 101.

LESSON: See More Teaching Tools on pages 116-117. <u>Ask, "When Jesus comes again, why will He come to the temple?"</u> Answer the question using the scriptures, Primary lessons, and sources (below) to teach.

• When the Savior comes again to begin the Millennium, He will come to a temple (*Gospel Principles*, chapter 43; Articles of Faith 1:10; *Primary 5*, lesson 30).

• We will do temple work in the Millennium. It will be a time of peace and joy and righteousness (*Gospel Principles*, chap. 44; Revelation 7:13-15; *Primary 7*, less. 46).

• My family and I can prepare for the Savior's coming by living to be worthy of temple blessings (*Gospel Principles*, chapter 43, 44, 47; *Primary 2*, less. 43; *Primary 7*, less. 25).

BITE SIZE MEMORIZE

And if U R faithful, ♥ hold, 👁 am with U until 👁 come - And verily, verily, 👄 say N2 U, 👁 come quickly.

D&C 34:11-12

ACTIVITY: When Jesus Returns the World Will Know Peace
("Lamb and the Lion" Millennium Match Game)

OBJECTIVE: Help children image what it will be like when Jesus returns, bring 1,000 years of peace to the earth.

TO MAKE: (1) *Copy, color, and cut out the lambs and lions (pages 95-98). (2) Option: If you want children to remain seated while choosing matches, write the letters A-P on the back of each lamb and lion, so children can call out the letters. (3) Laminate for durability. (4) Mount images on a poster paper (so they are not in order). Tape images face down with tape at the top, placing the lambs on the left and lions on the right.

TO INTRODUCE ACTIVITY:

• Tell children, "Before Jesus ascended into heaven, He told his apostles that He was to first return to our Heavenly Father until the time of his second coming. When He returns again He will return to the temple and bring in the millennium. The millennium is the thousand-year period when Jesus will reign on the earth. This will be a time of peace where Satan will be bound. Evil will not have

power. Even 'the lamb shall lie down with the lion.'" Place a lamb and lion on the board and talk about the difference in these two animals: The lamb is so gentle and small and the lion is large and dangerous. But when the millennium comes, the "lamb shall lie down with the lion," means there will be peace everywhere.

• Talk about the verse or sing the verse in the *Hymns* book, page 2, *The Spirit of God: "How blessed the day when the lamb and the lion shall lie down together without any ire."*

1. Tell children, "Let's play the Lamb and Lion Millennium Match Game to learn what will happen in this thousand years of peace when Jesus will reign on the earth.

2. Divide children into teams and have them take turns turning cards over and reading the Millennium event to make a match. <u>The first part of the sentence is on a lamb and the second part of the sentence is on a lion</u>.

3. Child can come up and point to a lamb and lion to make a match. Or, children can call out a letter (A-P written on the back of each lamb or lion) to identify their choices. Example, child can call out a letter from the lion side and a letter from the lamb side to make a match.

4. When a match is made, take the lamb and lion off and tape it to the side of the board away from the game.

5. Tell children that after the Millennium of 1,000 years, Satan will be set free for a short time and some people will turn away from Heavenly Father. Satan will build armies. The angels and hosts of heaven will cast him out forever. Then all the people who have ever lived on the earth will be judged and assigned to the kingdoms they have prepared for by the way they lived. The earth will be changed into the celestial kingdom.   - Source: *Gospel Principles*, chapter 43-44, 47

*All images can be printed in full-color or black and white with the *Primary Partners Sharing Time: The Temple* CD-ROM.

And if U R faithful, 🐝 + hold, 👁 am with U until 👁 come — And verily, verily, 👁 say N2 U, 👁 come quickly.

D&C 34:11-12

2 There will be no death.

2 Instead of death, we will be changed in the twinkling of an eye.

1 Disease will be taken from the earth.

1 There will be no sickness.

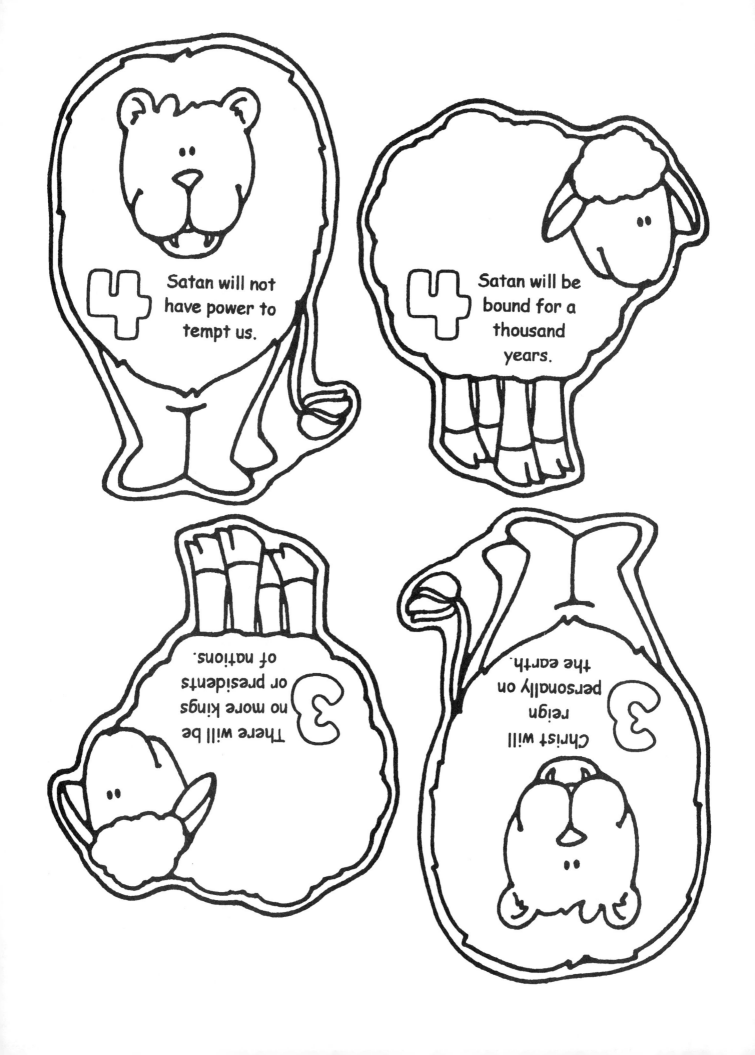

4 Satan will not have power to tempt us.

4 Satan will be bound for a thousand years.

3 There will be no more kings or presidents of nations.

3 Christ will reign personally on the earth.

6 Animals will
have no
enemies.

6 Animals that
now eat meat
will eat grass
and grain.

5 Christ will
teach us out
of the sealed
and lost
books.

5 Unrevealed
truths will be
revealed by
the Lord.

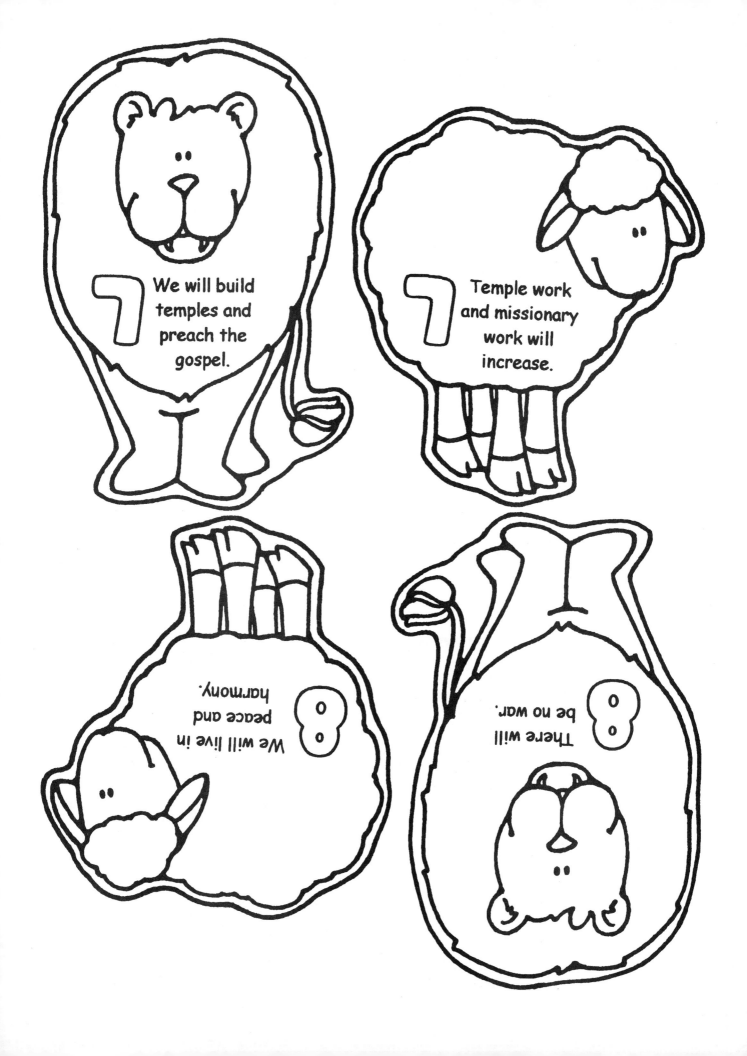

We will build temples and preach the gospel.

Temple work and missionary work will increase.

We will live in peace and harmony.

There will be no war.

BITE SIZE MEMORIZE

Who [shall] [abide] [stand] in his holy place? He [that] hath clean [hands], and a pure [heart].

Psalm 24:3-4

BITE SIZE MEMORIZE

And [I] [will] give N2 thee the [keys] of the [king]+dom of [heaven]: and whatsoever thou shalt [bind] on [earth] [shall] [be] [bound] in [heaven].

Matthew 16:19

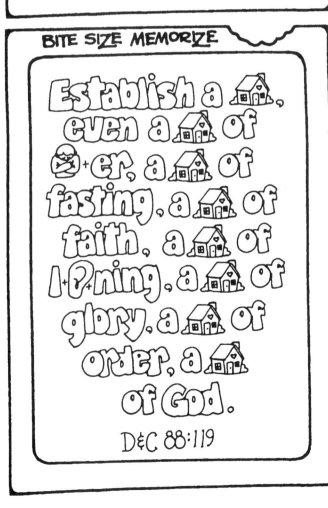

BITE SIZE MEMORIZE

Establish a [house], even a [house] of [pray]+er, a [house] of fasting, a [house] of faith, a [house] of l+[ear]+ning, a [house] of glory, a [house] of order, a [house] of God.

D&C 88:119

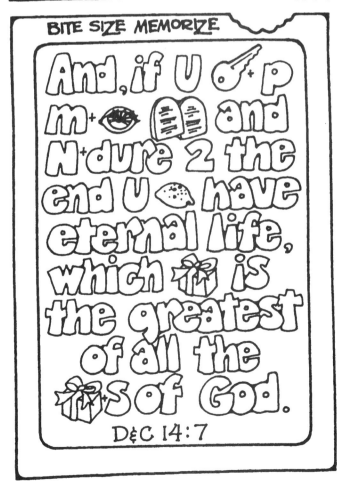

BITE SIZE MEMORIZE

And, if U [key]+p M+[eye] [commandments] and N+dure 2 the end U [shall] have eternal life, which [gift] is the greatest of all the [gift]s of God.

D&C 14:7

BITE SIZE MEMORIZE

Know ye [candy] t+[hat]
ye R the [temple] of
God, and t+[hat]
the [spirit] it of God
d+[well]+eth in U?
...4 the [temple] of God
is holy, which
[temple] ye R.

1 Cor. 3:16-17

BITE SIZE MEMORIZE

[eye] [command]+[hand] U,
all ye my
saints, 2
build a [house]
N2 me.

D&C 124:31

BITE SIZE MEMORIZE

And many nations
[shall] come, and say,
Come, let us go
[up] 2 the [mountain] of
the Lord,... and
he [will] teach us of
his ways, and
we [will] [walk] in
his [path]+s.

Micah 4:2

BITE SIZE MEMORIZE

And he [shall] [turn]
the [heart] of the
[father]+s 2 the [children],
and the [heart] of
the [children] 2 the
[father]+s.

Malachi 4:6

BITE SIZE MEMORIZE

He to[hat] hath my [tablets], and [hand]+peth them, he it is to [hat] [Love]+eth me.

John 14:21

BITE SIZE MEMORIZE

We [bee]+[leaf] to[hat] the 1ST [disc]+iples and ordin+[ants]+es of the Gospel R: 1st. Faith in the Lord [Christ]: 2nd. Repent+[ants]: 3RD. [baptism] by immersion 4 the remission of sins; 4TH. Laying on of [hands] 4 the [gift] of the Holy [dove].

Articles of Faith 1:4

BITE SIZE MEMORIZE

Let the [heart] of all my [children] rejoice, [owl]+who have ...built this [house] 2 my name.

D&C 110:6

BITE SIZE MEMORIZE

And if U R faithful, [bee]+hold, [eye] am with U until [eye] come – And verily, verily, [eye] say N2 U, [eye] come quickly.

D&C 34:11-12

MORE TEACHING TOOLS

The following Teaching Tools suggest more ideas for Sharing Time for
Themes #1-12 "THE TEMPLE" 2002 year.

We have made it easier for you to access all of the following Teaching Tools
without purchasing the eight *Primary Partners*—Primary manuals 1-7 activity books:
Primary Partners Nursery and Age 3, Volume 1 and 2
Primary Partners CTR-A and *Primary Partners CTR-B*
*Primary Partners Ages 8-12 New Testament, Old Testament,
Book of Mormon, and Doctrine and Covenants and Church History.*

We have combined all of the Teaching Tools suggested on the following pages
in one book and CD-ROM with full-color or black and white images.

To use the following Teaching Tools, simply copy the activities found in
the <u>eight</u> *Primary Partners* books (listed above), or the <u>one</u> *Primary
Partners Teaching Tools* book and CD-ROM (shown above):

• For small sharing time groups or family home evening, copy the activities at
the actual size (8 ½ x 11") to present and give as handouts.

• For large sharing time groups, enlarge the activities to show-and-tell.

Theme #1: I Love to See the Temple - Psalm 24:3-4

The temple is a house of God, a place of love and beauty.
I can feel the Holy Spirit there (D&C 109:12-20; *Primary* 1, lesson 26

TEMPLE IS WHERE VALIANT SAINTS SERVE THE LORD: (shown right)
Primary 7, lesson 42 Valiantville obstacle course (*Primary Partners*—New Testament, lesson 42).

I'll go inside someday to perform sacred ordinances that will prepare me to live with Heavenly Father again. I will make covenants and receive my endowment (Mosiah 5:5, *LDS Temples,* 14-19; *Primary 5,* lesson 35; *"Temple"* in the Bible Dictionary).

I WILL LIVE WORTHY FOR TEMPLE BLESSINGS: (shown left) *Primary 5, lesson 35* child's photo in temple frame (*Primary Partners*—D&C, lesson 35).

I WILL PREPARE TO GO INSIDE THE TEMPLE: (shown right) *Primary 7, lesson 7* I Have a Strong Spirit! I Can Say No! poster (*Primary Partners*—New Testament, lesson 7).

I will prepare myself while I am young to go to the temple. I must have a recommend to enter a dedicated temple (Alma 37:35; "My Gospel Standards"; *Primary* 3, lesson 3)

HEAVENLY FATHER HELPS ME OBEY: (shown left) *Primary 4, lesson 3* Commandment Concentration (*Primary Partners*—Book of Mormon, lesson 5).

I CAN BE A POSITIVE INFLUENCE ON FRIENDS: (shown right) *Primary 6, lesson 34* Peer Pressure cross match puzzle (*Primary Partners*—Old Testament, lesson 32).

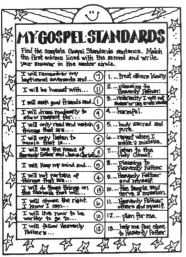

I WILL PREPARE: (shown right) *Primary 6, lesson 24* Follow Righteous Leaders Trust-and-Tell Game (*Primary Partners*—Old Testament, lesson 24).

LIVE WORTHY FOR PRIESTHOOD BLESSINGS: (shown left) *Primary 6, lesson 47* My Gospel Standards search (*Primary Partners*—Old Test., lesson 47).

*All of the Teaching Tools above are found in one book: **Primary Partners Sharing Time: TEACHING TOOLS: The Temple**. Also available on CD-ROM to print in color or black and white graphics.

Theme #2: My Family can be Together Forever
Through the Blessings of the Temple - Matthew 16:19

In the temple my family can be sealed together forever. Marriage in the temple is for eternity (D&C 132:19; *Gospel Principles*, chapter 38; *Primary 3*, lesson 35 (enrichment activity 1)

BIRDS OF A FEATHER STICK TOGETHER:
(shown left) *Primary 1, lesson 2* bird nest family fun (*Primary Partners*—Nursery, lesson 2).

LET'S BE TOGETHER FOREVER: (shown right) temple eternity wheel *Primary 3, lesson 35* temple eternity wheel (*Primary Partners*—CTR-B, lesson 35).

FAMILIES CAN BE TOGETHER FOREVER:
(shown below/right) *Primary 1, lesson 2* temple prep slide-show (*Primary Partners*—Nursery, lesson 2).

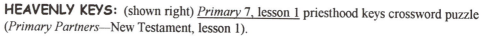

Temple ordinances are performed by priesthood authority (D&C 132:45-49; *Primary 5*, lesson 26, *LDS Temples*, 23-26).

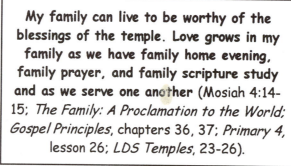

UNLOCK THE POWERS OF HEAVEN:
(shown left) *Primary 5*, lesson 26 priesthood keys reminder (*Primary Partners*—D&C, lesson 26).

HEAVENLY KEYS: (shown right) *Primary 7, lesson 1* priesthood keys crossword puzzle (*Primary Partners*—New Testament, lesson 1).

My family can live to be worthy of the blessings of the temple. Love grows in my family as we have family home evening, family prayer, and family scripture study and as we serve one another (Mosiah 4:14-15; *The Family: A Proclamation to the World*; *Gospel Principles*, chapters 36, 37; *Primary 4*, lesson 26; *LDS Temples*, 23-26).

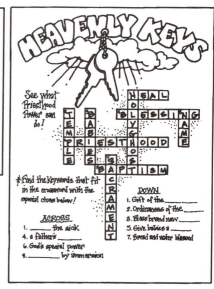

I CAN PREPARE FOR THE TEMPLE:
(shown left) *Primary 4, lesson 8* What Would Jesus Do? situation sack (*Primary Partners*—Book of Mormon, lesson 8).

*All of the Teaching Tools above are found in one book: **Primary Partners Sharing Time: TEACHING TOOLS: The Temple.** Also available on CD-ROM to print in color or black and white graphics.

Theme #3: The Temple Is the House of the Lord - D&C 88:119

When Jesus lived on the earth, He came to the temple in Jerusalem (Luke 2:22-52; John 8:2; *Primary 7*, lessons 5, 8)

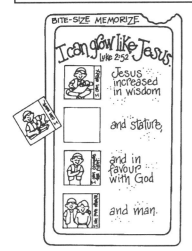

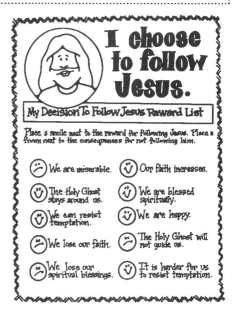

I CAN BECOME LIKE JESUS: (shown left) *Primary 7, lesson 5* Luke 2:52 bite-size memorize sticker poster (*Primary Partners*—New Testament, lesson 5).

I WILL FIND HAPPINESS AS I FOLLOW JESUS: (shown right) *Primary 6, lesson 23* Decision to Follow Jesus Reward List (*Primary Partners*—Old Testament, lesson 23).

After His resurrection, the Savior came to the Nephite temple in the land Bountiful. He taught and blessed the people there (3 Nephi 11; *Primary 4*, lessons 33, 35).

I HAVE A TESTIMONY OF JESUS CHRIST: (shown right) *Primary 4, lesson 33* love and gratitude journal (*Primary Partners*—Book of Mormon, lesson 33).

When the Savior comes to earth, He often comes to a temple. We can feel His Spirit there (D&C 110:1-10; 97:15-16; 109:5; *Primary 1*, lesson 26, account of Lorenzo Snow).

I WILL PREPARE FOR THE TEMPLE BY SHOWING RESPECT: (shown left) *Primary 7, lesson 8* respectful choices with stickers (*Primary Partners*—New Testament, lesson 8).

THE CHURCH OF JESUS CHRIST IS ON THE EARTH TODAY: (shown right) *Primary 2, lesson 42* Then and Now sticker poster (*Primary Partners*—CTR-A, lesson 42).

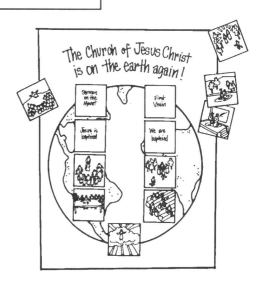

*All of the Teaching Tools above are found in one book: ***Primary Partners Sharing Time: TEACHING TOOLS: The Temple**. Also available on CD-ROM to print in color or black and white graphics.

Theme #4: The Temple Brings the Blessings of Heaven to Earth – D&C 14:7

The temple teaches us Heavenly Father's plan of salvation
(Gospel Principles, chapter 47; *Primary* 1, lesson 3).

BEFORE EARTH LIFE I CHOSE TO FOLLOW JESUS: (shown right) *Primary 2, lesson 4* premortal life puppet show (*Primary Partners*—CTR-A, lesson 4).

HEAVENLY FATHER'S PLAN IS FOR ME: (shown left) *Primary 6, lesson 1* Plan of Salvation story board and quiz (*Primary Partners*—Old Testament, lesson 1).

HEAVENLY FATHER TRUSTS US TO FOLLOW HIS PLAN: (shown right) *Primary 3, lesson 2* heaven road map (*Primary Partners*—CTR-B, lesson 2).

The temple is a house of learning and inspiration
(D&C 97:10-16; Primary 5, lesson 26).

I CAN LIVE WITH HEAVENLY FATHER AGAIN: (shown left) *Primary 5, lesson 23*, connected kingdoms (*Primary Partners*—D&C, lesson 23).

A picture of the temple reminds me I am a child of God.
If I keep the commandments, I can live with Him someday
(Romans 8:16-17; Primary 6, lesson 12, enrichment activity 6).

I AM A CHILD OF GOD: (shown left) *Primary 1, lesson 3* paper dolls with heavenly and earthly home (*Primary Partners*—Nursery, less. 3).

WE ARE ALL HEAVENLY FATHER'S CHILDREN: (shown left) *Primary 2, lesson 3* heavenly family photo (*Primary Partners*—CTR-A, lesson 3).

I CAN FOLLOW JESUS AND OBEY: (shown above) *Primary 2, lesson 30* heavenly treasure hunt (*Primary Partners*—CTR-A, lesson 30).

I WILL RETURN TO MY HEAVENLY HOME: (shown right) *Primary 6, lesson 4* I Can Return maze (*Primary Partners*—Old Testament, lesson 4).

All of the Teaching Tools above are found in *one* book: **Primary Partners Sharing Time: TEACHING TOOLS: The Temple. Also available on CD-ROM to print in color or black and white graphics.*

Theme #5: My Body Is a Temple - 1 Corinthians 3:16-17

I will keep my mind and body sacred and pure, and I will not partake of things that are harmful to me. (*Primary* 3, lesson 14; *Primary* 5, lesson 24, enrichment activities).

I AM BLESSED WHEN I EAT HEALTHFULLY: (shown right) *Primary 3, lesson 14* Word of Wisdom choices pockets (*Primary Partners*—CTR-B, lesson 14).

I WILL SAY "NO" TO HARMFUL AND "YES" TO HEALTHFUL: (shown left) *Primary 5, lesson 24* Word of Wisdom voting ballot (*Primary Partners*—D&C, lesson 24).

GOOD FOOD MAKES MY BODY STRONG: (shown left) *Primary 1, lesson 2* Daniel eats good food eating pocket (*Primary Partners*—Nursery, lesson 2).

I WILL KEEP THIS LAW OF HEALTH: (shown right) *Primary 6, lesson 40* Word of Wisdom Choices match puzzle (*Primary Partners*—Old Testament, lesson 40).

> **I will only listen to music that is pleasing to Heavenly Father. I will only read and watch things that are pleasing to Heavenly Father** (*Primary* 3, lesson 38; *Primary* 6, lesson 16, enrichment activities).

I WILL STAY AWAY FROM EVIL: (right) *Primary 6, less. 16* Look Ahead Decision Drama (*Primary Partners*—Old Testament, lesson16).

SACRED HYMNS BRING BLESSINGS: (left) *Primary 5, less. 14* "Note"able Hymns secret code message (*Primary Partners*—D&C, less. 14).

> **I will use the names of Heavenly Father and Jesus reverently. I will not swear or use crude words** (Exodus 20:7; *Primary* 3, lesson 43; *Primary* 7, lesson 41). **I will dress modestly to show respect for Heavenly Father and myself** (*Primary* 5, lesson 44, activity 2).

I WILL HONOR THE NAMES OF HEAVENLY FATHER AND JESUS: (shown left) *Primary 3, lesson 43* reverent mouth pop-up picture (*Primary Partners*—CTR-B, lesson 43).

I CAN BE TONGUE TIGHT: (shown above/left) *Primary 7, lesson 41* sweet speech word search (*Primary Partners*—New Testament, lesson 41).

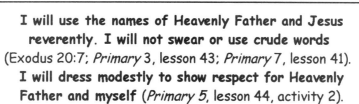

ESEPLA	P L E A S E
KAHTNUYO	T H A N K Y O U
UYLIEVOO	I L O V E Y O U
ROSRY	S O R R Y
MROFVGIEE	F O R G I V E M E
ESEEUCXM	E X C U S E M E
BYULSESO	B L E S S Y O U

All of the Teaching Tools above are found in one book: **Primary Partners Sharing Time: TEACHING TOOLS: The Temple. Also available on CD-ROM to print in color or black and white graphics.*

Theme #6: Temples Are a Sign of the True Church - D&C 124:31

> **Moses and the children of Israel had a tabernacle, a temple they carried with them**
> (*LDS Temples*, 52-61; Exodus 33:7; D&C 124:38; "Tabernacle" in the Bible Dictionary).
> **Solomon built a temple in Jerusalem** (1 Kings 6:1; *Primary 6*, lesson 31).

MOSES FREED THE ISRAELITES SO THEY COULD WORSHIP:
(shown right) *Primary 6, lesson 19* Priesthood Power/Egyptian Plagues crossword puzzle (*Primary Partners*—Old Testament, lesson 19).

> **The Nephites had temples**
> (2 Nephi 5:16; Jacob 1:17; Mosiah 2:1-7; 3 Nephi 11:1)

NEPHITE TIME AND ZION TIME:
(shown left) *Primary 4, lesson 37* Prayer Then and Now Challenges obstacle course game (*Primary Partners*—Book of Mormon, lesson 37).

> **Joseph Smith restored temple blessings in the latter days**
> (D&C 124:39-40; *Primary 5*, lesson 25, 26, 35).

ANGEL MORONI'S GOOD NEWS MESSAGE:
Primary 5, lesson 3 (shown left) Moroni's match game (*Primary Partners*—D&C, lesson 3).

I CAN "BEAR" MY TESTIMONY OF THE TRUE CHURCH:
(shown far left) *Primary 7, lesson 37* find the secret message poster (*Primary Partners*—New Testament, lesson 37).

PROPHET JOSEPH SMITH RESTORED THE GOSPEL OF JESUS CHRIST: (shown right) *Primary 5, lesson 37* tribute scripture search (*Primary Partners*—D&C, lesson 37).

*All of the Teaching Tools above are found in one book: **Primary Partners Sharing Time: TEACHING TOOLS: The Temple**. Also available on CD-ROM to print in color or black and white graphics.

Theme #7: Temples Bless Heavenly Father's Children
Throughout the World Today - Micah 4:2

The pioneers worked hard and sacrificed to build temples
(D&C 97:12; 109:5; *Primary* 5, lessons 35, 44).

PIONEERS TRAVELED TO ZION AND SACRIFICED TO BUILD THE TEMPLE: (shown right) *Primary 5, lesson 38* Zion or Bust! handcart checklist (*Primary Partners—*D&C, lesson 38).

Members of the Church today make sacrifices to go to the temple (*Primary* 5, lesson 25, enrichment activities, 4).

I WILL WORK HARD TO SERVE LIKE PIONEERS: (shown left) *Primary 5, lesson 41* pioneer word find puzzle (*Primary Partners—* D&C, lesson 41).

PREPARING FOR MY LIFE'S MISSION: (shown right) *Primary 6, lesson 18* Mission statements match game (*Primary Partners—*Old Testament, lesson 18).

Theme #8: We Serve Others
Through Temple Work - Malachi 4:6

In the temple, ordinances are performed for our families and others who have died without receiving ordinances such as baptism, endowments and sealings (D&C 138:53-58; *Primary* 5, lesson 34).

I AM GRATEFUL TO BE BAPTIZED AND FOR TEMPLE ORDINANCES: (shown right) *Primary 5, lesson 12* Ordinances Opportunity game (*Primary Partners—*D&C, lesson 12).

I can prepare to serve in the temple by learning about my ancestors and doing family history work (D&C 138:47-48; *Gospel Principles*, chapter 40; *Family Home Evening Resource Book*, lesson ideas, "Genealogy").
I can write my personal history and write in my journal (1 Nephi 9; 19:1; *Family Home Evening Resource Book*, lesson ideas, "Journals").

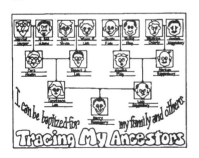

I CAN BE BAPTIZED FOR THE DEAD: (shown left) *Primary 5, lesson 34* Tracing My Ancestors pedigree chart (*Primary Partners—*D&C, lesson 34).
FAMILY I LOVE YOU: (shown right) *Primary 1, lesson 25* family tree with stickers (*Primary Partners—*Nursery, lesson 25).

*All of the Teaching Tools above are found in <u>one</u> book: ***Primary Partners Sharing Time: TEACHING TOOLS: The Temple.*** Also available on CD-ROM to print in color or black and white graphics.

Theme #9: I Will Live Now to Be Worthy to Go to the Temple and Serve a Mission - John 14:21

> **I will pay my tithing**
> (*Primary* 3, lesson 42, *Primary* 7, lesson 24).

I WANT TO PAY MY TITHING: (shown right) *Primary 3, lesson 42* tithing bills match game (*Primary Partners*—CTR-B, lesson 42).

> **I will be honest with Heavenly Father, others, and myself** (*Primary 2*, lesson 34; *Primary 6*, lesson 14).

I WILL KEEP GOOD PROMISES: (shown above) *Primary 6, lesson 14* Honesty Pays Blessings Bucks board game (*Primary Partners*—Old Testament, lesson 14).

I WILL TELL THE TRUTH: (shown above/right) *Primary 2, lesson 34* Trevor and Trina Truth sack puppets (*Primary Partners*—CTR-A, lesson 34).

> **I will do those things on the Sabbath that will help me feel close to Heavenly Father** (*Primary 2*, lesson 37;

I WILL CHOOSE RIGHTEOUS SABBATH ACTIVITIES: (shown right) *Primary 7, lesson 14* Sabbath Search maze (*Primary Partners*—New Testament, lesson 14).

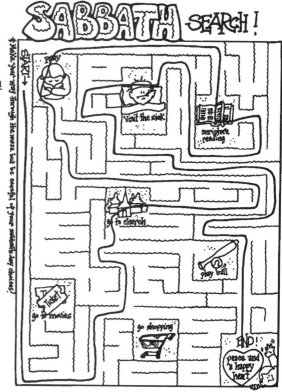

*All of the Teaching Tools above are found in one book: *Primary Partners Sharing Time: TEACHING TOOLS: The Temple.* Also available on CD-ROM to print in color or black and white graphics.

Theme #9: I Will Live Now to Be Worthy to Go to the Temple and Serve a Mission

I WILL KEEP THE SABBATH DAY HOLY: (shown right) *Primary 5, lesson 41* Sabbath Day Decision Drama or Draw (*Primary Partners*—D&C, lesson 41).

I will seek good friends and treat others kindly (*Primary* 1, lesson 33; *Primary 7*, lesson 20).

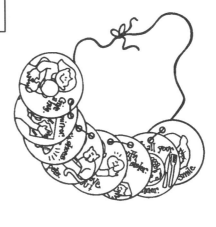

I WILL TREAT OTHERS KINDLY: (shown left) *Primary 1, lesson 46* kind deeds necklace (*Primary Partners*—Nursery, lesson 46).

I WILL SHOW LOVE: *Primary 7, lesson 20* (shown left) Love Lingo Bingo game (*Primary Partners*—New Testament, lesson 20).

I WILL DO GOOD UNTO OTHERS: (shown left) *Primary 3, lesson 44* Golden Ruler (*Primary Partners*—CTR-B, lesson 4).

I WILL SHOW LOVE UNTO OTHERS AS I SERVE: (shown right) *Primary 6, lesson 10* My Circle of Love Spin-and-Serve game (*Primary Partners*—Old Testament, lesson 10).

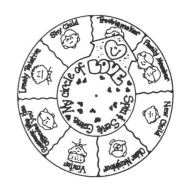

I will share the gospel with others (*Primary* 3, lesson 25; *Primary* 4, lesson 17).

I WILL SHARE AND CARE: (shown left) *Primary 1, lesson 34* Good Samaritan Show-and-Tell (*Primary Partners*—Nursery, lesson 34).

I WILL BE A TRUE FRIEND TO JESUS AND OTHERS: (shown right) *Primary 6, lesson 29* Fishing for a Friend spin-and-tell (*Primary Partners*—Old Testament, lesson 29).

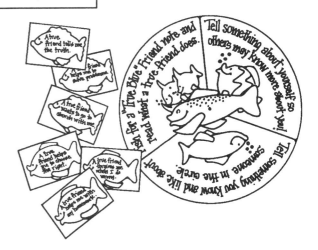

*All of the Teaching Tools above are found in one book: ***Primary Partners Sharing Time: TEACHING TOOLS: The Temple.*** Also available on CD-ROM to print in color or black and white graphics.

Theme #10: I Prepare to Go to the Temple as I Follow Heavenly Father's Plan for Me – Articles of Faith 1:4

See Alma 37:33; *Primary 6, lesson 6*; 1999 and
2000 *Outline for Sharing Time and the Children's Sacrament Meeting Presentation.*

I HAVE FAITH IN THE LORD JESUS CHRIST:

I WILL LIVE THE GOSPEL OF JESUS CHRIST: (shown right) *Primary 6, lesson 6* Faith Footsteps goal flip chart (*Primary Partners*—Old Testament, lesson 6).

I WILL THINK OF JESUS: (shown left) *Primary 7, lesson 29* Testimony Building Blocks puzzle (*Primary Partners*—Old Testament, lesson 29).

I WILL REMEMBER MY BAPTISMAL COVENANTS:

I WILL FOLLOW JESUS: (shown right) *Primary 4, lesson 10* Commitment Connection rhyme and reason (*Primary Partners*—Book of Mormon, lesson 10).

I PROMISE AND HEAVENLY FATHER PROMISES: (shown far left) *Primary 3, lesson 13* baptism two-sided puzzle (*Primary Partners*—CTR-B, lesson 13).

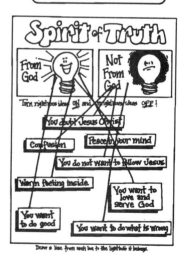

I WILL DEVELOP SPIRITUAL STRENGTH: (shown above) *Primary 6, lesson 25* Sink or Swim slide-show (*Primary Partners*—Old Testament, lesson 25).

I WILL LISTEN TO THE HOLY GHOST:

JESUS SPEAKS TO ME THROUGH THE HOLY GHOST: (shown right) *Primary 6, lesson 27* Find the Spirit of Truth cross match (*Primary Partners*—Old Testament, lesson 27).

*All of the Teaching Tools above are found in one book: ***Primary Partners Sharing Time: TEACHING TOOLS: The Temple.*** Also available on CD-ROM to print in color or black and white graphics.

Theme #10: I Prepare to Go to the Temple as I Follow Heavenly Father's Plan for Me

I WILL CHOOSE THE RIGHT. I KNOW I CAN REPENT WHEN I MAKE A MISTAKE:

I WILL MAKE GOOD CHOICES: (shown right)
Primary 6, lesson 2 Choices and Consequences match game (*Primary Partners—Old Testament, lesson 2*).

I WILL MAKE RIGHT CHOICES: (shown below)
Primary 2, lesson 2 choose-and-match puzzle (*Primary Partners—CTR-A, lesson 2*).

I CAN REPENT AND BE FORGIVEN:
(shown right) *Primary 3, lesson 22* repentance wheel (*Primary Partners—CTR-B, lesson 22*).

I WILL FOLLOW JESUS: (shown left) *Primary 3, lesson 1* "Chews" the Right gum ball machine (*Primary Partners—CTR-B, lesson 1*).

*All of the Teaching Tools above are found in one book: **Primary Partners Sharing Time: TEACHING TOOLS: The Temple.** Also available on CD-ROM to print in color or black and white graphics.

Theme #10: I Prepare to Go to the Temple as I Follow Heavenly Father's Plan for Me

MY TESTIMONY WILL GROW AS I STUDY THE SCRIPTURES, PRAY, GO TO CHURCH, AND FOLLOW THE PROPHET (2 Nephi 31:14-21; 32:8-9; Primary 5, lesson 46).

STUDY AND PRAYER STRENGTHEN MY TESTIMONY: (shown right) *Primary 5, lesson 46* TESTIMONY word race (*Primary Partners—D&C, lesson 46*).

I CAN GROW CLOSER TO HEAVENLY FATHER: (shown left) *Primary 2, lesson 10* prayer rock (*Primary Parnters—CTR-A, lesson 10*).

MY TESTIMONY GROWS AS I STUDY, PRAY, GO TO CHURCH, AND FOLLOW THE PROPHET:

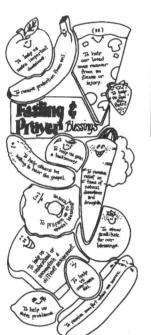

FASTING AND PRAYER INCREASE MY FAITH: (shown left) *Primary 6, lesson 38* Fasting and Prayer Blessings post-and-present (*Primary Partners—Old Testament, lesson 38*).

THE GOSPEL OF JESUS CHRIST IS TRUE: (shown right) *Primary 6, lesson 41* Valiant Testimony board game (*Primary Partners—Old Testament, lesson 41*).

LISTEN AND OBEY: (shown left) *Primary 5, lesson 31* The Prophet Guides Choice Consequences cross match (*Primary Partners—D&C, lesson 31*).

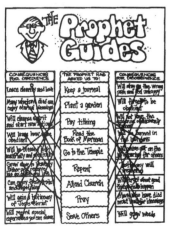

*All of the Teaching Tools above are found in one book: ***Primary Partners Sharing Time: TEACHING TOOLS: The Temple.*** *Also available on CD-ROM to print in color or black and white graphics.*

Theme #11: I Am Thankful for Temple Blessings - D&C 110:6

I am thankful to know that Heavenly Father has a plan for my family to be together
(D&C 59:23; *LDS Temples*, 74-75; *Primary 3*, lesson 35, enrichment activity 1)

LET'S BE TOGETHER FOREVER: (shown left) *Primary 3, lesson 35* temple eternity wheel (*Primary Partners*—CTR-B, lesson 35).

FAMILIES ARE SPECIAL: (shown right) *Primary 2, lesson 6* missing family puzzle (*Primary Partners*—CTR-A, lesson 6).

Temple blessings help me feel happiness and peace in my life and in my home
(*Primary* 2, lesson 1; *Primary 4*, lesson 38).

I WILL BE HAPPY AS I MAKE RIGHT CHOICES: (shown left) *Primary 4, lesson 24* Value-Pack of Good Choices (*Primary Partners*—Book of Mormon, lesson 24).

I FEEL HAPPY AS I LIVE THE TEACHINGS OF JESUS: (shown right) *Primary 4, lesson 38* Happy Choices match game (*Primary Partners*—Book of Mormon, lesson 38).

HAPPINESS COMES FROM CHOOSING THE RIGHT: (shown left) *Primary 2, lesson 1* CTR happiness wheel (*Primary Partners*—CTR-A, lesson 1).

Temple blessings help me know that Heavenly Father and Jesus Christ love me. I can show my gratitude to them
(D&C 78:18-19; *Primary 2*, lesson 24).

I LIKE TO REMEMBER JESUS: (shown right) *Primary 1, lesson 40* sacrament manners match game (*Primary Partners*—Nursery, lesson 40).

*All of the Teaching Tools above are found in <u>one</u> book: ***Primary Partners Sharing Time: TEACHING TOOLS: The Temple.*** Also available on CD-ROM to print in color or black and white graphics.

Theme #12: When Jesus Comes Again,
He Will Come to the Temple - D&C 34:11-12

When the Savior comes again to begin the Millennium, He will come to a temple
(*Gospel Principles*, chapter 43; Articles of Faith 1:10; *Primary 5*, lesson 30).

MISSION OF JESUS CHRIST: (shown left) *Primary 7, lesson 35* premortal, mortal, and postmortal life review game and Moses 1:39 bite-size memorize poster (shown right) (*Primary Partners*—New Testament, lesson 35).

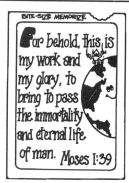

We will do temple work in the Millennium.
It will be a time of peace and joy
and righteousness
(*Gospel Principles*, chapter 44;
Revelation 7:13-15; *Primary 7*, lesson 46).

I WILL PREPARE BY LIVING RIGHTEOUSLY:
(shown below) *Primary 6, lesson 36* Millennium Match Game (*Primary Partners*—Old Testament, lesson 36).

PARABLE OF THE SHEEP AND GOATS: (shown left) *Primary 7, lesson 27* Sheep and Goat Situation Slap Game (*Primary Partners*—New Testament, lesson 27).

*All of the Teaching Tools above are found in one book: **Primary Partners Sharing Time: TEACHING TOOLS: The Temple**. Also available on CD-ROM to print in color or black and white graphics.

Theme #12: When Jesus Comes Again, He Will Come to the Temple

My family and I can prepare for the Savior's coming by living to be worthy of temple blessings (*Gospel Principles*, chapters 43, 44, 47; *Primary 2*, lesson 43; *Primary 7*, lesson 25).

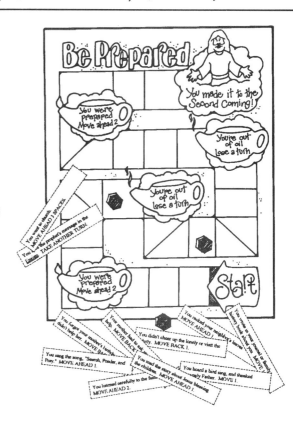

I WILL PREPARE TO MEET MY SAVIOR JESUS CHRIST: (shown left) *Primary 5, lesson 30* strong heart mobile (*Primary Partners*—D&C, lesson 30).

I WILL PREPARE TO SEE JESUS: (shown right) *Primary 7, lesson 25* Be Prepared board game (*Primary Partners*—New Testament, lesson 25).

I WILL BE READY WHEN JESUS COMES AGAIN: (shown left) *Primary 7, lesson 46* Second Coming Checklist (*Primary Partners*—New Testament, lesson 46).

I WILL PREPARE: (shown right) *Primary 6, lesson 24* Follow Righteous Leaders Trust-and-Tell Game (*Primary Partners*—Old Testament, lesson 24).

*All of the Teaching Tools above are found in one book: **Primary Partners Sharing Time: TEACHING TOOLS: The Temple**. Also available on CD-ROM to print in color or black and white graphics.

ACHIEVEMENT DAYS for Girls Ages 8-11

Here are <u>two</u> fun-filled, information-packed books with matching CD-ROMs focusing on each of the Achievement Days goals. Leaders, you will never be at a loss when it comes to choosing activities or projects to make goal achievement memorable.

You can make these activities simple or elaborate. Whatever your choice, you'll all be in for a great time! Start each activity with an invitation to create interest, for a year's worth of "go"al get 'em activities!

Each CD-ROM allows you to print the patterns from your computer in black and white. The latest book *Primary Partners: Quick-and-Easy Ways* (detailed below) allows you to print images in full color as well as black and white.

SUMMARY OF BOOK AND CD-ROM (shown right):
Primary Partners Achievement Days:

MOTIVATIONAL PARTIES: Pop Into the Future!, Soar to Success!, Dad and Me Western Jamboree, Mom and Miss Pig-nic, and Burstin' with Pride!

24 GOAL ACTIVITIES: <u>Arts and Crafts</u>: Let's Make Pop-ups! You're on Stage! <u>Education and Scholarship</u>: Wishin' in the Wishin Well Be a Jelly Bean Reader <u>Family History</u>: My Family Tree and Me Journal Jazz! <u>Family Skills</u>: I Can Cook! Super Sitter Basics <u>Health and Personal Grooming</u>: An Apple-a-Day the Healthy Way Closet Class! <u>Hospitality</u>: Friends Forever! Let's Be Pen Pals! <u>Outdoor Fun and Skills</u>: Ladybug Gardening Fun! Nature Photo-rama! <u>Personal Preparedness</u>: I Can Eat an Elephant! My Cents-able Savings Plan <u>Safety and Emergency Preparedness</u>: I Can Be Safe First Aid Station <u>Service and Citizenship</u>: Hop to it! Service That Grand Old Flag! <u>Spirituality</u>: B.E.A.R.S. (<u>Be Enthustiastic About Reading Scriptures</u>) Home Sweet Home <u>Sports and Physical Fitness</u>: Three Cheers for Good Sport! Freta Frog's Fitness Plan

SUMMARY OF BOOK AND CD-ROM (shown left):
Primary Partners Quick-and-Easy Achievement Days:

MOTIVATIONAL PARTIES: Zap Boredom with Zippy Achievement Days, Buttons and Bows Daddy Daughter Date, Mom and Me Fahion Show, Quarterly Activities: Fishing for Success!, Clowning Around Carnival, Hat s Off to You!, and You're a Star!

24 GOAL ACTIVITIES: <u>Arts and Crafts</u>: Drawing Fun! I'm "Sew" Happy! <u>Education and Scholarship</u>: Coloring My Life with Knowledge School is Cool! <u>Family History</u>: Scrap Happy Scrapbook Fun! "Meet My Ancestor" Spotlight <u>Family Skills</u>: Create Heart and Fun Shaped Bread Do Sparkle and Shine Jobs in a Jar <u>Health and Personal Grooming</u>: Beauty Shop Talk Healthy Food Fun! <u>Hospitality</u>: Mending/Keeping Friendship It's Party Time! <u>Outdoor Fun and Skills</u>: Splish, Splash Water Fun/Safety Campfire Cooking <u>Personal Preparedness</u>: Turn Over a New Leaf Bloom Where You're Planted <u>Safety and Emergency Preparedness</u>: Ladybug, Ladybug Fly Away Home Fire Safety <u>Service and Citizenship</u>: Scatter Sunshine Senior Service Entertain Children While Parents Serve <u>Spirituality</u>: Gospel Standards Hel Me Sunday Fun Activities <u>Sports and Physical Fitness</u>: Heart Smart Exercise Workout Flip Over Old Fashioned Games!

Preview of *File Folder*
FAMILY HOME EVENINGS
book and CD-ROM
You'll Find 12 Themes to Use for Primary Lessons,
Primary Sharing Time, and Family Home Evening
by Ross and Guymon-King

T H E M E S :
HEAVENLY TREASURES: Follow the
Straight and Narrow Path
SEEDS OF FAITH: My Testimony Is Growing
ANGEL TELLS OF TWO BIRTHS: John and Jesus
LET'S CELEBRATE the Birth of Jesus
CREATING ME: I'm Trying to Be Like Jesus
FISHERS OF MEN: Jesus Choose 12 Apostles
BLESSED BEATITUDES:
Jesus Gave the Sermon on the Mount
THE GIFTS HE GAVE:
Tell Me the Stories of Jesus
SERVICE WITH A SMILE: Jesus Performed Miracles
CHOOSE THE RIGHT: Jesus Is Our Light
CAPTAIN OF OUR SHIP: Jesus Is Our Life Savior
IN HIS STEPS: Spotlighting the Life of Jesus

Below is a sample of one
presentation that is ideal
for the Follow the
Prophet Theme #12
Primary sharing time.
Simply enlarge visuals for
large groups. Other
themes shown above are
great to teach children
about Jesus.
**CAPTAIN OF OUR
SHIP:** Jesus Is Our Life
Savior presentation
(right).
GAME: S.O.S. Save Our
Ship: Jesus Is Our Life
Savior scripture reading
and decision making
(shown left).
THOUGHT TREAT:
Jesus Is Our Life Savior
doughnuts or Lifesaver
candy.

PRIMARY PARTNERS
CLIP ART ON CD-ROM

PREVIEW: More than 500 Images (samples below) + 2 Free Fonts (shown left and above)

Jennette Guymon-King puts a wealth of her fun and creative images at your fingertips for all your clip art needs. Print images in black and white or color. Use this tool for all your creative projects. Use for Primary classes, sharing time, singing time, Sunday School classes, family home evening, ward newsletter, Achievement Days (balloons shown right), and more. Make posters, reward stickers, badges, invitations, cards, story visuals, object lessons, awards, signs and banners, games, and puzzles. Use to decorate a ward newsletter. Choose from a variety of Book of Mormon, Bible, and Doctrine and Covenants themes, dozens of borders, headlines, family and baptism illustrations, and much, much more. Each image is available in a variety of formats for Windows computers.

Mary H. Ross, Author and
Jennette Guymon-King, Illustrator
are the creators of
PRIMARY PARTNERS BOOKS & CD-ROMS
Lesson Match Activities and More:
Nursery and Age 3 (Sunbeams) Vol. 1 + CD-ROM
Nursery and Age 3 (Sunbeams) Vol. 2 + CD-ROM
CTR A and CTR B Ages 4-7 + CD-ROMs
Book of Mormon Ages 8-11 + CD-ROM
Old Testament Ages 8-11
New Testament Ages 8-11 + CD-ROM (color)
Doctrine and Covenants Ages 8-11 + CD-ROM (color)
Achievement Days, Girls Ages 8-11 + CD-ROM
Quick-and-Easy Achievement Days Ages 8-11 + CD-ROM (color)
Primary Partners: Clip-Art on CD-ROM (500 images-color)
Singing Fun! (each year's theme) + CD-ROM (color)
Sharing Time (each year's theme) + CD-ROM (color)
Sharing Time TEACHING TOOLS (each year's theme) + CD-ROM (color)
FAMILY HOME EVENING BOOKS & CD-ROMS:
File Folder Family Home Evenings + CD-ROM
Home-spun Fun Family Home Evenings 1 + CD-ROM
Home-spun Fun Family Home Evenings 2 + CD-ROM
YOUNG WOMEN BOOKS & CD-ROMS:
Young Women Fun-tastic! Activities Manual 3
Young Women Fun-tastic! Activities Manual 1 + CD-ROM
Young Women Fun-tastic! Activities Manual 2 + CD-ROM (color)

MARY H. ROSS, Author

Mary Ross (shown left) is an energetic mother and has been a Primary teacher and Achievement Days leader. She loves to help children and young women have a good time while they learn. She has studied acting, modeling, and voice. Her varied interests include writing, creating activities and children's parties, and cooking. Mary and her husband, Paul, live with their daughter, Jennifer, in Sandy, Utah.

JENNETTE GUYMON-KING, Illustrator

Jennette Guymon-King (shown right) has studied graphic arts and illustration at Utah Valley State College and the University of Utah. She served a mission in Japan. Jennette enjoys sports, reading, cooking, art, gardening, and freelance illustrating. Jennette and her husband, Clayton, live in Riverton, Utah. They are the proud parents of their daughter, Kayla Mae, and sons, Levi and Carson.